Best wishes from —

THE IRISH
DETECTIVE
IN YORKSHIRE

GERRY O'SHEA

The Irish Detective in Yorkshire
ISBN SB Edition: 9 781910 097182
ISBN HB Edition: 978-1-910097-33-5

This edition printed and bound in the Republic of Ireland by
Lettertec Irl. Ltd,
Springhill House,
Carrigtwohill
Co. Cork
Republic of Ireland

www.selfpublishbooks.ie

DEDICATED TO THE THIN BLUE LINE
AND
THE IRISH DIASPORA

CONTENTS

INTRODUCTION

Sometimes I think fighting crime is as simple as ABC. Maybe not exactly, but the initials provide a good grounding and starting point for any police officer faced with the task of successfully investigating a crime:

A – accept nothing.
B – believe no one.
C – check everything.

I was born in 1952 in a rural part of the Republic of Ireland. My schooling and early working life was largely untouched by crime or by discrimination issues. Like many Irish people before me and like many now in these recessionary times, I took the emigration route to England as a young man. It was not an easy option then and it still presents problems to the thousands of young Irish people following in my footsteps. My experience may prove useful to them.

This book details my trials and tribulations as a young Irish man getting to grips with my different lifestyle while steadfastly holding on to my own beloved culture. I will take you on a journey from my Irish farmyard to the West Yorkshire Metropolitan police force. How I overcame hurdles to progress through the ranks to become a senior detective. I will also give an insight into some of the many cases I had to deal with and how I became known as The Irish Detective and how my annual appraisals described me as one of the best detective inspectors in the force. I was commended at the highest levels on dozens of occasions by Chief Constables, High Court Judges, Crown Court Judges, Coroners and Magistrates for such things as bravery, courage, integrity, professionalism and the high quality of my investigatory skills.

32 years later I retired from the force having undergone a maturity of character and outlook caused by a most demanding way of life.

Can anyone blame me for becoming somewhat cynical after a lifetime of people telling lies, cheat and do the most unspeakable acts, motivated chiefly to benefit or save their own selfish skins.

This book is about my particular journey through a demanding and interesting career and looks at it from my perspective. Any thoughts or opinions are solely of my own and I do not seek to represent anyone else. I do not try to present any deep thinking, psychological examination of the police service or life itself – what you see is what you get.

I have deliberately anonymised some of the individuals involved, so as not to cause any undue anxiety or embarrassment to other persons. In a true and factual account of events though, it is impossible to completely sanitise my account. Any intrusion of privacy is minimal and intended for the greater good by showing the effects of emigration and serious crime on everyone involved in it.

I hope you enjoy reading the book.

Chapter 1

Irish Roots

January 1973. "How's it going?" – shouted my neighbour, farmer Mikey Boran, as I waited with my suitcase outside my house at Deerpark near the small country town of Castlecomer, in Southern Ireland. It was 7am on a cold winter morning, and Mikey was riding past on his bicycle going to check on his cows. Seeing me dressed unusually smartly and with a small brown suitcase at my side prompted another shout. "Are you going somewhere, Gerry?" – he enquired.

I've never been a morning person and I didn't feel too much like engaging in a conversation at this time of the day. Especially as I had already told Mikey at least a dozen times that I was going to England on Monday. I said: "I'm going to England, Mikey, remember, I told you..." "Oh Janey Mac, sure I forgot all about that!" – said Mikey – "Look after yourself now!"

Mikey was one of two middle-aged bachelor brothers who owned a small farm near our house. They were genuine decent people and very good neighbours. Their lives revolved around their farm

4

and were not complicated in any way by external influences such as marriage or any other events outside of their farm. The farthest either of them had ever been was to Dublin about 60 miles away. Mikey had made one trip there to a greyhound race some years earlier and he still lived on the details of that trip as if he had gone round the world.

As youngsters, my friends and I would spend as much time as we possibly could helping out on the farm. It was fun for us playing with the animals and the brothers enjoyed our company and appreciated the little bit of help we gave. I would often spend my entire school summer holidays working on the farm – milking the cows, feeding the animals and picking potatoes in the fields. Mikey's brother, Pat, was in charge of finances and he would pay me 2 pounds a week, but I would have done it for nothing.

I think Mikey and Pat had actually influenced me to be heading for a distant shore on that January morning. I saw how their lives revolved around their farm and whilst they had a good happy life, I wanted to see more of the world than my small country town.

Castlecomer had a population of about one thousand people at that time. Four streets coming to a cross-road in the centre basically made up the town. Residents had a pride in the town and it was kept neat and tidy. It is very picturesque with its main square of Georgian houses, and lime trees on each side being particularly pleasing to the eye. The only cinema had long since shut down. There were a few shops and a small supermarket. There were 10 pubs which was way out of proportion for such a small town, but, as there was little else to do in the form of entertainment, all of the public houses did very well.

I was born 2 miles outside of the town in the Deerpark on 1st April 1952. Being born on April Fools' Day has not made me a fool, but it may have had some influence on my outlook on life. I don't take life over seriously, realising there is more important things to life than everyday material things. What does it matter if you don't have much money or if it is cold or raining. If you are healthy and happy, then that is what is important.

The Deerpark was a closely knit hamlet of 18 houses situated beside the Deerpark colliery – one of the largest anthracite coal mines in Europe at the time. The Deerpark cottages were built for miners working in the colliery. My father John worked in the colliery, above ground, as a store manager. My mother Lily stayed at home and was the perfect mother for looking after the family. I was the 3rd oldest of six children – Joe, Marie, George, Chrissie, Lucy and myself.

We lived in a large detached house in the countryside. For several years my mother supplemented the family income by running a small shop from the house. She sold sweets, pop and ice cream to the neighbours and passing miners going to and from the colliery.

Almost every family in the area were given a local nickname, and to many people we were known as the 'Pop Shea's' because of the goods sold in the shop.

George and Lucy both suffered from cerebral palsy and were both seriously handicapped. They could not walk or talk or do anything for themselves. My mother was their full-time carer as well as looking after her husband my father and her other four children. In those days there was very little support to families such as ours with disabled children. My mother devoted her whole life to caring for George and Lucy until she died aged 83 years. It was only in the later years of her life that she got some support from government agencies.

In 1994 she was nominated and won the Irish National Carers Association 'Carer of the Year' award. It was her proudest moment when she received the award from the Irish President Mary Robinson. If anyone ever deserved recognition for devoting their life to the care of others, it was my mother.

I attended the Boys' National School at Castlecomer. There was no school transport in those days. Along with my Deerpark friends I walked the 2 mile journey to school each morning and again back home in the afternoon. When I say 'every day', I mean – almost every day. Sometimes we would midge school for a day and go exploring in the countryside. Climbing trees to collect hazelnuts and fishing in the river Deen were great fun. Climbing onto the back of the steam train service to the coal mine was also more exciting than school. My school attendance records though were better than most of my friends. Even at that young age I knew it was important to have an education.

Corporal punishment in those days in Ireland was a daily event at school. The teachers would punch, kick or hit us with a stick without much reason. I was a polite and well-behaved pupil, but that did not always mean I would get away unscathed. I remember one day the teacher sent me up to the field to get him a stick from a tree to beat the pupils. Thinking I was in his good books, I got him a nice long flexible stick, like a cane. He was not happy that I had been quick enough, so he broke in the new stick by giving me three lashes across the legs.

The fact was, it didn't really matter if you were 'good' or 'bad'. What actually mattered was what kind of mood the teacher was in. The only pupils who were not beaten were those ones we called the 'townie pets'. Those were the boys from families of influential business people, shopkeepers or farmers. One of my first lessons learnt, was born from this. In Ireland it did not matter what you knew or how you behaved. It mattered only who you were. If you were well off or had a priest or a nun, or someone who played county-level hurling in your family, you would be all right and have a chance of a decent job. None of these applied to me, so I was always going to have to work hard and probably emigrate to make anything of myself.

I don't think getting a slap or crack of a stick from the teachers actually did any harm to us. We were never sexually or mentally abused. We knew where we stood, and we could handle it. Maybe it made us stronger later in life. I am not advocating brutality in any sense, but in many areas of society today there is no such thing as discipline of any type, and it is not a good thing.

My only complaint about it was the sense of injustice about it all. I was a good pupil – I did my homework, I was respectful to the teachers and I worked hard. Yet, for no apparent reason, I would feel the knuckles of the teacher on my head and a crack of the stick on my legs regularly. That sense of injustice and unfairness has stayed with me all of my life, and I have gone out of my way to address those issues whenever I could. Especially on behalf of vulnerable people who had difficulty in helping themselves.

When I was 14 years old, I left school and was looking for a job. My prospects were limited in this small Irish town with very little opportunities. As I said earlier, we were not a prominent family in the town, we had no clergy family members, and I could not play hurling to save my life. The colliery was the main employer in the area, and as a storeman my father was 'on the staff'. I wasn't sure exactly what that meant, but I knew he was proud of it, and he got to wear a collar and tie to work. He told me he had got me a job in the mine, as was the norm for most young men of my age at that time. I can't say I was looking forward to it, but I had been expecting it. There was no application process, and I had no interview to undergo, it was all sorted out by my dad.

My elder brother Joe had gone down the mine after leaving school. He had been involved in an accident when some of his fingers had been blown off in an explosion and narrowly escaped drowning when an underground tunnel flooded on another occasion. He had left the mine soon after and went to England.

I had also heard the various anecdotes of the dangers of working in the mine, and I knew it was not going to be a bed of roses. Several miners had lost their lives in the mine, and everyone knew how dangerous it was. I think my father must have exaggerated my age, as I was only 14 years when I first went down the mine. It was unusual for someone of my age to go straight underground to work, but the colliery was in decline and the only job for me was as a labourer, or 'jobber', underground.

I will never forget the first morning when, armed with my helmet, lamp and shovel, I went down the tunnel into the mine. One of the miners who was a neighbour of mine was given the task of looking after me. The clerk at the Time Office logged me in before I went down the tunnel as he did with all the other miners. This was so that I could be accounted for if I didn't return at the end of the shift. The other miners had their own permanent brass fob with their number on it, but the Time Clerk only gave me a temporary pass as he obviously suspected I wouldn't be staying too long. He was a friend of my father, and I know he later told my father off for sending me down the mine so young.

This mine was only a short walk from our house, and so I was familiar with its environment. Though, I wasn't familiar with life underground. With the other shift miners, I trudged for hundreds of yards down the long dark tunnel to a place called the Big Flat. Then we branched off into a small tunnel and walked for another half hour or so until we were in total darkness and wet ground. I was told to clean up with another young miner, and we shovelled stone into trams and then pushed them forward. It was hard physical work. We sat in the cold and wet and had our sandwiches while we breathed in the dust that filled the air.

At the coalface the experienced miners crawled on their belly and, using a pick and shovel, dug the coal out. They spent most of the shift in that position. My neighbour who was looking after me told me he would take me to the coalface the next day, which I took more as a threat than a treat. There was no such thing as a canteen. We ate our sandwiches where we worked, watched by rats as big as small dogs. Oh how I longed to be back in school! A good hiding by the teacher would be better than this.

I got home that night and told my father my career as a miner was over. I wouldn't be going back. He tried to persuade me to go again the following day, while he would try to get me another job in the colliery, but there was no way I was going down there again. The shortest career as a miner ever! But I came away with an unquestionable admiration for those miners who made their living by going underground every day. They were incredible men, the toughest of the toughest. They worked so hard in such terrible conditions, day after day.

The following day my father told me he had got me a job 'overground'; I was to be a clerk in the mining office based in Castlecomer. And so my new life as a mining clerk began. The people who worked in the office saw themselves as a step above me. Most of them were from the town and were educated better than me. It certainly had never been known that a lad from the Deerpark had worked in any office. It's fair to say that I did not fit into the office scene. No one really spoke to me and I hated every second of it. My options were running small, but I decided I would not be in the mining office on week two.

I'd heard a garage service station up the street was looking for an assistant. Not being one to let the grass grow under my feet, I walked up at lunchtime and spoke to the manager, Martin O'Grady. Half an hour later, after a successful interview, I was handing in my notice at the mining office. After going through two jobs in one week I was hoping my career in Kings Garage would be more successful. Martin told me my wages was 2 pounds 13 shillings and 4 pence in old money. That was for working seven days in the week with a half-day on Wednesday.

Martin and his family were great to work for and I learned a lot of things in my time at the garage. I learned how to deal with customers and how to repair cars and bicycles. Working in the town and meeting lots of other people really expanded my social skills, and I made lots of new friends. I bought a racing bicycle and used to cycle the 2 miles to and from work each day. At the end of the week I gave my mother all of my wages and she gave me back 2 shillings and 6 pence, which, along with a few tips from customers kept me going all week and financed my second-hand racing bike. I used to have my lunch every day at my aunt Peggy Cantwell's house in Maryville in the town. I was now well established in the 'townie circles'.

After 12 months of selling petrol and making minor repairs to cars and bikes, I was ready for a change. One of my customers at the garage worked on the staff of Kilkenny Products Ltd, a structural steel manufacturing company based 12 miles away in the city of Kilkenny. He arranged an interview and put in a good word for me. Another example of who you knew was important, not what you knew.

At the age of 16 years, after a successful interview, I began work at Kilkenny Products. From £2-13-4d a week I was now earning the huge amount of between £12 and £15, depending on productivity. The big problem with working in the Products was getting there and back. I would cycle the 2 miles from the Deerpark to Castlecomer, then I would thumb a lift into Kilkenny and back again after work. I started work at 8am and finished at 6pm. In order to get to work on time I had to leave home at 6am and often did not get home until 9pm because sometimes it was difficult to get a lift. I often had to walk the 12 miles or hitch a lift on the back of a tractor trailer.

After a few months of hardship I had saved some money from my wage and went to Walls motorcycle shop in Kilkenny and bought a brand new Honda 125cc with shining chrome metalwork. It had high handlebars and a backrest. I felt like a Hell's Angel on Route 66 as I rode about on it. As sod's law would have it, the factory relocated to premises in Castlecomer soon after I had bought the motorcycle. Still, the motorcycle made my working day much shorter. It also extended my ability to travel further afield and make new friends. It became my new 'babe magnet' and I had no shortage of girlfriends. I travelled to other towns such as Ballinakill, Ballyragget and Durrow and made new friends.

I started in the Products as a general labourer. That meant I was really a 'dogsbody' who had to do all the lifting, sweeping and other menial tasks. After a while I progressed to be a painter. This must have been the most unskilled painting job in the whole world. With a group of others, I would paint the steel structures in red oxide paint. The more we painted, the more wages we got. We also got up to all sorts of mischief. Basically, we painted in red oxide paint anything that didn't run away from us. We also painted each other. So much so that our overalls were so thick in paint, they would stand up on their own when we took them off.

It was hard and physical work in the Products. The foreman who went by the name of Dargle was a tyrant and a bully who appeared to thrive on making our lives a misery. After some time I was promoted to be a welder, which was seen as a skilled job and I got a pay rise of 3 pounds a week.

A new textile factory called 'Comer Yarns' had opened in the town and a lot of my friends were now working there. I'd heard it was a good civilised place to work with good wages, so I applied for a job. The interview process was very thorough, but I was successful. In November 1971 at the age of 19 years I began working at Comer Yarns. I was a textile machinist with a wage of £20 per week.

Life was good in the Mills. It was a warm, clean environment to work in. Most of the workforce was about my own age, and we all got on famously well. The supervisors and managers were all decent people who treated us well, not like my previous foreman in the Products. In return for a decent wage and being treated properly we all worked very hard.

It was just as well I had not wanted to remain a coal miner as the colliery had shut down in 1969. A lot of the older miners found it difficult to get other employment and many of them never worked again. But the new industry in the town was boosting the local economy, and the younger miners who could adapt found themselves working in much cleaner and safer environments. To many people it was a blessing in disguise to see the end of the coal mine.

In addition to the Mills and the Products, two other factories had opened – a brick manufacturing plant and a caravan building factory. This meant the social life aspect of the town was good, especially at weekends. However, our social lives all seemed to revolve around alcohol. There was very little else to do. Long drinking sessions, followed by late night dances was the norm at weekends. In those days we all drank far too much and no one was bothered about drink driving laws or about the bad effects of alcohol. It was only several years later that drink driving became regarded as antisocial and was treated more seriously by the public and the Gardaí.

I had started going into the local pubs and drinking alcohol since I was about 15 years old. All of my friends did the same and no one seemed to care. My only concern was that my father should not find out. He was a drinker himself, but I knew he would be very unhappy to know I was drinking at such a young age. I dealt with this by having a glass of Coke on the bar table alongside my pint of ale. If my father appeared in the rear pool room, where we congregated, I would drink the Coke.

On the occasions when I went home drunk, I would go straight to my bedroom, where my parents would not observe me. My mother knew I was drinking because she would often check on me and see if I was alright. She would tell me not to drink, but of course I thought I knew better. In fairness, there really was nothing else to do.

We were a law-abiding family. There was no way any of us would get into trouble with the law. We were brought up to respect other people and their property. Getting into any type of trouble not only would let our parents down, but also would bring great shame on the family in the small community in which we lived.

When I was 18 years old I did have a minor brush with the law. I was stopped driving my Honda motorcycle in the town of Carlow, about 12 miles from where we lived. Unfortunately, I did not have a driving licence and I received a summons in the post a short time later. I did not tell my parents because I knew they would be very disappointed in me, and on the due date I set off to Carlow court on my own.

This was the first time anyone in my family had been in a courtroom and I was very embarrassed. I sat in the public seating area, while a Garda officer told the district judge of stopping me and asking for my driving licence. The judge then spoke to me. I didn't have to go into the dock, I just stood up where I was. He said to me: "If you tell me you have a licence at home, I will let you off". While probably most people might have said "it's at home" and gone on their way, I was too frightened and too honest to lie. I said – "I don't have a licence", and the judge then fined me five shillings. Paying five shillings did not bother me in the least, but I was concerned what my parents would say if they found out. I have to say that my parents would never raise a hand against me or any other family member or even shout in anger. Their disappointment with me would be enough to worry me.

The local weekly newspaper, The Carlow Nationalist, usually reported everything that happened in the Carlow area and not a lot ever happened. You couldn't let a loud fart as it would be in the paper. There was only one newsagents shop in our town, so, the following week, as soon as 'The Nationalist' went on sale, I went to Holohan's shop and bought a copy. To my horror, my name appeared in the court notes. I went back into the shop and I bought all the copies of the paper that they had. I don't know what the newsagent thought was going on as I left clutching more than 30 copies of the local rag. It was a good job it wasn't in the Kilkenny People as it had a much larger circulation and I would have been broke to buy them all. My efforts at covering my tracks were futile and in due course my parents and everyone else realised I was a hardened criminal. After all my worry my parents were not really concerned at all, and shrugged it off as just one of those things. It was though another lesson in life for me – to stay on the right side of the law.

The church was an important part of my life as I grew up. Indeed, it was an integral part in the lives of everyone who lived in the area, 95% of the local population were Roman Catholic with the remainder belonging to the Church of Ireland. We all got on very well with our Protestant neighbours, and there was no conflict or tension between us – unlike the situation in the north of Ireland where 'the Troubles' were at its height. We all went to Mass on Sunday mornings. Often us young lads and girls would be nursing sore heads after a late night drinking session, but that made no difference. We would not miss Mass. It wasn't that we were very religious, it was just our culture and the thing to do. Again, we knew that if we didn't go to Mass, we would be letting our families down and the neighbours would talk. We had our own corner in the church where we would sit together and laugh and snigger at the previous night's events in between the prayers.

In those days the large Church of the Immaculate Conception in Castlecomer would be packed at every mass. Not so now, as the congregation has dwindled, for whatever reasons. It is a beautiful church, both outside and inside, and well worth a visit, if you ever find yourself in the town. I was baptised in that church as were all my family and friends. There I received my first confession, my first communion, and confirmation. I got married there and we had all our family funerals in that church. I expect my demise will also be mourned, or celebrated, there as well.

I remember having a comical encounter with the church when I was about 12 years old. The parish priest, Father O'Keefe, would regularly come to our school and talk to us about religion. He drove a new car and he lived in the large parochial priest house on the hill, overlooking the town. He had a housekeeper who made all his meals for him. I also knew that people were very generous and placed plenty of money in his church collections. On this particular day, Father O'Keefe asked the boys in my class if any of us would like to become a priest like him. I considered all the plus points – the big house, new car, housekeeper and plenty of cash and I thought, yes, that looks okay, so I put my hand up. I didn't mean anything serious by putting my hand up. I was just being polite and daydreaming. I wasn't volunteering to be a priest, and I didn't realise the parish priest was on a recruitment drive.

About a week later I was at home when Father O'Keeffe arrived at our door. I overheard him talking to my mother saying he had come to see me as I was interested in joining the priesthood. That was the last thing on my mind, so I opened the back door and ran up the field as fast as I could. Looking back, I saw my mother calling me with the astonished priest beside her. I stayed up the fields for about four hours until I was sure I wasn't going to be taken away to become a priest. Maybe I should have stayed where I was. Who knows what would have happened – Bishop O'Shea in the big house with a housekeeper? You never know!

As I mentioned earlier, the pay in the Mills was very good. I had enough money to give some to my mother for housekeeping, run my motorcycle and enjoy an active social life. As a family we were comfortably off. We only had our father's wage and whatever us working children contributed, but we seemed to do okay. My father had a VW Beetle, and we were first in the Deerpark to get a television and a telephone. Our house was always busy with people coming in to use the telephone. It became a little bit inconvenient when they came in the middle of the night to ring the doctor.

Our new Philips black and white television set was also very popular. Most evenings the wall outside our living room window would be full of local youngsters peering in the window to watch the cartoons. Luckily, we only had one channel to watch, so no one got upset by channel switching. It wouldn't work nowadays, with all the channels to choose from.

The opportunity came for me to buy my first car. My sister Marie's boyfriend, later to be her husband, Ted Ruth, was selling his car. It was a lovely blue coloured Ford Cortina. Ted sold me the car for a bargain price of £80. I never had any lessons or driving tuition.

I just picked it up as I went along and it was easy enough on the quiet country roads. There was only one set of traffic lights in the area. They were 12 miles away on The Parade in the middle of Kilkenny city and I stayed well away from them until I became confident with my driving.

The junction had been relatively accident-free until they erected the traffic lights and then there were minor accidents almost daily. I remember myself and my good friend Bimbo Nolan spending hours on The Parade studying the traffic lights and considering how best to negotiate our way through them.

In 1972 I was 20 years old. Life was good. I was the proud owner of a big Ford Cortina and had a good job in the Mills. I was still looking to the future though, and I could not see how I could better myself and remain at home. I applied to join the Irish police – the Garda Síochána – and had undergone an entrance exam in Dublin. I had passed in all areas except the Irish language paper. I had failed by a few marks. My Irish language wasn't great. I had only learnt basic Irish at school. I didn't speak it and no one I knew ever spoke it. I was invited to re-sit the exam, but I knew it was pointless until I brushed up on my Irish language, and I didn't have the appetite to do that. I didn't appreciate why Irish was required when hardly anyone in the area spoke it. Nowadays, any EU resident can join the Gardaí with no Irish, and even with poor English.

In my own mind I thought I would have to emigrate, like so many Irish youth before me. I thought America or Australia sounded good, but there was also a big problem as I was a home bird. I loved my family and friends, and I was very comfortable in my local surroundings. I knew it would be difficult to leave them and stay away. America and Australia were another world away. Even the UK was a long way off in those days before budget airlines.

I had spoken to my parents, and while they would prefer me to stay at home, they realised and agreed I didn't have much chance of a good future in Ireland. One of the reasons behind their support of emigration were 'the Troubles' taking place in the North of Ireland. My father was afraid they would lead to all-out civil war, and he was afraid I would get caught up in it. I think that his fears were realistic because the ranks of the IRA were growing in the Republic. The events of Bloody Sunday in January 1972 led to huge support for the IRA and boosted recruitment. Even in our quiet part of the country feelings were running high. But I wasn't all that keen myself to be involved in any sort of paramilitary fighting.

An opportunity to advance came my way out of the blue. Comer Yarns was going from strength to strength and the company was looking at ways to develop further. In those days, Bradford in West Yorkshire was one of the leading textile manufacturing cities in the world. The company had the brilliant idea of increasing their sales by opening an outlet in Bradford. They were looking for someone to go to Bradford on a six-month contract to help get the outlet off the ground. I put myself forward on the thinking that I could go and 'have a look' and, if I didn't like it, I could come back to my old job. I was selected to go to Bradford, and here I was now, on this freezing morning in January 1973, waiting outside my house to be picked up to go to the airport.

While I was excited by the prospect of my new adventure, I was also a bit sad. I was glad it was very early in the morning and no one, except Mikey Boran, was out to see me off. I had said goodbye to my mother and father, but they had stayed inside. They would not want me to see them upset and I didn't want anyone to see me with weepy eyes. That same scenario would be repeated many times over the coming years as I returned home for holidays and family events. I would always arrange it so that my wife Marion and I, and our four boys, would leave for the airport or ferry very early in the morning, before we would see anyone. We would always be upset at leaving, but at least no one could see us and make it even worse.

As Mikey bid me farewell and disappeared up the road on his bicycle, I dried the tears from my eyes and saw my lift to the airport had arrived. I sat in the rear seat of the shiny new Ford Capri as we travelled the 65 mile journey to Dublin airport. The car was driven by Martin Bennett and the front seat passenger was Tom Byrne. Mr Bennett was a manager in the Mills while Mr

Byrne was a factory floor supervisor. I knew Tom reasonably well from the factory, but I didn't know Martin that well as he worked in the office and I did not have much contact with him.

They talked business most of the time, and occasionally included me in the conversation. We spoke about the Bradford project and Mr Bennett told me there was a lot of hard work to be done to get it off the ground and he had high expectations of me. I thought to myself then, I hope I can deliver. We arrived at Dublin airport and caught an Aer Lingus flight to Leeds Bradford Airport. It was my first time on an aeroplane, and I was anxious not to show my inexperience.

Church of the Immaculate Conception, Castlecomer

Barrack Street, Castlecomer

Comer Yarns, Castlecomer

Deerpark

CHAPTER 2

HELLO YORKSHIRE

When we landed at Leeds Bradford Airport, Mr Bennett got a rental car while I had my first look at Yorkshire. It was several degrees colder than I was used to, and the airport was fairly busy. Little did I know then that in the coming years I would become a frequent traveller at the airport and would be as familiar with the area as I was of my birthplace.

As we drove into Bradford, it was lunchtime, so Mr Bennett stopped at a pub serving food. It was the large Tudor style Barrack Tavern Pub on Barkerend Road – now Habib's Restaurant. I had lunch and a pint of bitter ale for the very first time. The ale was awful and nothing like what I'd been used to. I should have stuck to soft drinks like my colleagues. After lunch we made the further five minute drive to the Comer Yarns factory in Florence Street. It was a small set up, consisting of some offices and a warehouse. There was a staff of five, consisting of a manager, Mr Appleton, and four others who were involved in selling the yarn produced in Ireland.

I was to work in the warehouse preparing the yarn in what is called a 'warping process', to make it more attractive to buyers and ready for weaving process. They all seemed very nice, although I couldn't really understand the Yorkshire accents, and, I'm sure, they didn't understand me either.

It had been arranged that I would stay in digs at a boarding house in Shipley, about 6 miles away. In the early afternoon, Mr Bennett, Tom and myself set off to Shipley in the hire car. I knew I had to make my way back to the factory for 8am the following day, so I did my best to try to memorise the route. It was a futile effort, it was a big city, and every road looked just the same. Every street was jammed full of cars and I'd never seen so much traffic in my life. The nearest I had ever seen to it was when a large funeral procession would pass our house on the way to church. There were textile mills everywhere with chimneys belching out black smoke into the sky. Except the smoke didn't go into the sky – it hung around like low black cloud. Now I knew where the phrase 'dark satanic mills' came from. Most of the buildings, especially those in the city centre, were covered in black soot.

When we arrived at Bradford Road in Shipley, I said goodbye to Martin and Tom and made my way into the guesthouse. The owner, Mrs Turner, was expecting me and made a fuss to make me feel welcome. She asked me various questions to which I replied in my strong Irish accent: "yes Ma'am, no Ma'am, three bags full,

Ma'am"… She said – "Call me June" and I said "okay Ma'am", but went on calling her 'Ma'am', all the time I was there.

She was fascinated by my accent and at how courteous and mannerly I was, and would call her family and other guests to marvel at how I spoke. She said she had never been called 'Ma'am' before. I didn't mind the attention she gave me, it made me feel good. She would stack my plate high with food, and then sit there watching me eat, like if I was a monkey in a zoo. She spoiled me rotten, but I played up to it and loved it.

Mrs Turner wrote down directions and bus numbers for me to find my way to work the next day. Then I realised I didn't have an alarm clock and I was worried that the following morning I would sleep in. I'd never been good at getting out of bed and usually relied on my mum to call me. I decided to walk into Bradford city centre and buy an alarm clock. Although it was about 8pm, I reckoned the shops would still be open. After all, the only newsagent's shop in Castlecomer stayed open until 10pm. Surely it would be the same here!

It was pretty much a straight road into Bradford, and I walked the several miles' journey getting into town at about 9pm. To my surprise, all the shops were closed. I walked from street to street, getting hopelessly lost in the process, until I eventually found an open shop with clocks in the window. I went inside and saw a number of people were sat down, playing some type of game. I went to the lady in charge and said I want to buy one of those alarm clocks in the window. She looked at me as if I had landed from Mars and said: "You can't buy those clocks, love. This is a bingo hall, and they are the prizes". I made a hasty retreat and got a taxi back to my digs.

I did manage to get up on time the next morning and, after Mrs Turner had filled me up with cornflakes and a cooked breakfast, I took my first venture on the city's buses. I got to the city centre easily enough. Getting across the middle of town and getting my bus up Leeds Road was a different matter. I had great difficulty in working out the subway system and I felt like a rabbit popping in and out of a burrow. Eventually I got to work a couple of hours later than scheduled. The staff were very understanding and appreciated the problems I had in finding my way around the new city.

Soon after I arrived at work, the manager, Mr Appleton, sent for me and I went to his office. What he told me really shattered me. After Mr Bennett and Tom had dropped me off the previous day, they had carried on driving to Lancashire, where they had further business. Unfortunately, the car had crashed and Tom had been killed. I felt so bad for his family in Ireland, and I suppose I also thought myself lucky that I had not been in the car. That evening I went with Mr Appleton to Lancashire, where I paid my last respect to Tom in a funeral home. It was a real tragedy to happen to such a lovely man. What a bad start to my new life in the UK.

I then began the routine of living and working in a new city and a new country with a very different culture. The hard part was that I knew absolutely no one in the place, and I was still struggling to find my way around. Some of the staff at Comer Yarns were good to me and invited me out on occasions. The textile foreman, a middle-aged man called Fred, was especially good to me. He drove a three-wheeled Reliant Robin and would drive me about to show me the area. I had never seen a three-wheeled car before, and was afraid it would tip over. It wasn't exactly a trendy car be seen in, and I always felt a bit embarrassed when people stared at us.

At weekends, Fred played an organ at a local working men's club. He took me along a few times with him. I had only heard an organ played in church before, and, to be honest, Fred's gig wasn't too dissimilar. Still, it got me out and about and meeting people. I must have appeared as an organ roadie to the old dears in the club.

One day I told Fred I was going to go to mass on Sunday and I asked him where the nearest Catholic Church was. He told me he was also a Roman Catholic and went to mass. He said he would pick me up on Sunday morning and take me to mass with him. As good as his word, he picked me up early on Sunday morning and we drove to a church in the Thornbury area. During the celebration of 'Mass' I was intrigued to see that it was all much different to what I'd been used to back home. Then I looked at one of the leaflets and saw that it was actually a Church of England service that I was in. After the service I felt a bit uneasy and hoped nobody told the Pope about me. I felt like a petrol car that had been filled up on diesel! Somehow I don't think poor old Fred was all that religious…

We were now ready to expand our operations at the mill and ready to appoint several more warehouse and textile staff. The manager allowed me to be involved in interviewing some of the candidates. We interviewed a young man called Taz Singh for a machinist job. Taz was from an Indian family. And an experienced textile machinist. I liked him from the outset. I told Mr Appleton I thought he was the best applicant and he was given the job. Taz was about my age and we got on famously well straightaway. He became my best friend. We were a bit of an odd couple as Taz spoke with an Indian accent, and I spoke with a strong Irish accent. Communication could be a problem, and we would regularly be telling each other to speak slower and clearer. Taz's background was a bit similar to my own; his family were very close and he had a closely knit community around him. Taz and I remained close friends for many years. He even visited Ireland with me a few times, and regarded himself as an honorary Irishman.

I was now keeping myself busy and getting to grips with some of the facilities available to me. I worked five days a week at the mill.

I had a part-time job most evenings as a security officer, visiting various factories and offices in a small van with an Alsatian guard dog. I also worked on Saturdays and Sundays at another textile mill in Shipley. Sometimes travelling to Shipley on a weekend was a problem so I would sleep in the warehouse on a Saturday night. In the little spare time I had I also attended night classes, studying maths and English language. I took a typing course and studied computers, which was being tipped as the big thing of the future. I attended swimming lessons and also went to weekly judo and karate courses. Every moment of every day was filled with something to do.

Things were going well in my job at Comer Yarns, and productivity was good. That had a knock-on effect of boosting production at the plant, both here and in Castlecomer, and it was good to know I was helping the folk back home.

CHAPTER 3

TWENTY ONE TODAY

In April 1973 I celebrated my 21st birthday in Bradford. I missed having all of my Irish friends and relatives – particularly my parents – around me, but by now I had amassed a large group of new friends, and they all helped me to celebrate it in style. In that same month Seamus Mealy, another worker from the Castlecomer plant, had come across to Bradford to work with me, and soon I would also be joined by my hometown girlfriend.

Seamus was about my own age. He had been a friend of mine back in Ireland and we had worked together in the textile mill. He quickly fitted into the workings of the Bradford plant. Seamus was a great worker and added tremendously to the work being achieved in the mill. We had a great social and working life and he is still a great friend of mine.

We became well-known in the local pubs and we played pool and darts with the pub teams. Although we both found ourselves in a somewhat alien and different environment, we made a huge effort to integrate into our new surroundings and it worked. It is important to retain ones' own culture, but it is also very important that immigrants make the effort to integrate – as it makes life so much easier. Seamus was to stay in Bradford for about five years before he returned to live permanently in Ireland, but I know he enjoyed his stay in the UK.

Seamus and myself stayed in a number of guest houses, but we found them a bit expensive and restrictive for two young men coming home late at night – often a bit tipsy. We decided we would be better off in our own house, so we rented a house at Steadman Terrace, a few minutes' walk from our place of work at Comer Yarns. We shared the house with a couple of students at Bradford University – the leaders of the future! We all got on very well together and had a great time. One difference we had was the manner in which we relaxed. Seamus and I would go out and have a few drinks in the local pubs, while the students would stay in the house with a few cans of beer and smoke cannabis all evening. We would get home somewhat inebriated and they would be totally spaced out talking gibberish. It was just not in our culture to take drugs of any sort.

I was still getting to grips with some new aspects of living in Bradford. There was a very large Asian community in the city. That did not bother me one iota. I did not have a prejudicial or racist bone in my body. In fact, as an immigrant, I was aware of having a lot in common with the Asian community. There were Asian shops everywhere selling Asian wares. Most of the cafes and restaurants were run by Asians and mainly dealt in curries and other spicy foods. I had no experience of eating spicy food whatsoever. A bit of pepper on my meal would be enough to have me blowing steam.

My very first encounter with eating curry came soon after I had arrived in the city. I went out one night on my own to explore. I went up Leeds Road where there was an abundance of public houses and restaurants. I had a few drinks in the pubs and then felt hungry. My meal of choice after a few drinks was always chicken and chips, and so I set off looking for some. There was many eating places, but they were all basic curry houses and did not do chicken and chips. Eventually, at the Evergreen Restaurant, I was now really hungry. The waiter said he didn't do chicken and chips, so I asked him what he did do. He said in his Pakistani accent – "Chicken and chapattis, sir…" I thought this was simply a breakdown in communication and what he's actually saying is 'chicken and chips', so I ordered it.

I paid and sat at a table in the restaurant while the waiters whispered together at the counter and eyed me with suspicion. I was then served something in a dish, along with some type of wraps. I waited patiently for several minutes for the waiter to bring me a knife and fork, but none was forthcoming. I looked at another table and saw a couple were eating the same dish with no knife and fork. There were tearing strips off the wrap and scooping from the dish. That's a strange way of carrying on, I thought, but here it goes. I took some chapatti and scooped some chicken from my dish. Unfortunately, the chicken was covered in curry sauce and it burnt the mouth off me. I gasped in fright and had a coughing fit while trying to catch my breath. The waiter brought me some water which I devoured in one gulp. I couldn't possibly eat this stuff, but I was in an awkward situation as the waiters were still staring at me. I tried another bit, but again it took my breath away and burnt my mouth. When the waiters were looking, I pretended to eat by chewing a bit of the chapatti on its own, and, as soon as they took their eyes off me, I was gone through the door in a flash... Taz Singh introduced me properly to curries in the coming months and I am now a gourmet of Asian cooking to the point where I eat far too much of the stuff.

Going out in Bradford was much different to what I'd been used to. In Ireland, our social life revolved around going to the pub. Here in Bradford, I still went to the pubs, but I also went to the cinema, to concerts and to shows in the theatre. I went ice skating, played snooker and pool. I went to soccer matches and rugby games. I watched speedway racing and stock car racing at Odsal Stadium. Across the road, at the Richard Dunn Sports Centre I played five-a-side football, badminton and squash. This kept me busy and fit as well. In my home town we went out in jeans and jumpers, but in the city it was a real dressing up job. Everyone made a special effort. The boys wore suits, shirts and ties, and the girls were dressed up to the nines.

I had a friend called Tony, who was a Teddy Boy. He and his friends dressed in 'Teddy Boy' gear – 'brothel creepers', 'drainpipe' trousers, a jacket and a shirt and a narrow strip of tie, all in the most outlandish colours. They tried to get me to join them, but I was never cut out to be a Teddy Boy. They were amazing at the rock and roll dancing and jiving. My dancing experience was limited to the town hall in Castlecomer where I would shuffle along to the slow numbers, and try to disguise the fact that I was born with two left feet.

Bradford was also a violent place to socialise. A lot of the young men carried flick knives. Mainly it was just part of their 'gear', but knives were often used in fights as well. It was commonplace to see fights inside and outside pubs on busy weekend nights. Back in Ireland we would never think of carrying a knife. Why would anyone want to use a knife?

Outside the Old Crown pub in Ivegate at closing time it looked like a war zone. Gangs fighting and a dozen police officers trying to separate them. Mind you, the police were not slow in handing out a bit of the violence themselves to the troublemakers. I was never involved, but it did make for great late night entertainment. In the main my friends and I managed to steer away from trouble. Sometimes people would try to pick a fight with us because of our Irish accents and Taz's Indian background. We had a few skirmishes, but we could always hold our own. We were no pushovers.

I now had lots of friends in Bradford and I kept myself very busy. However, I still missed home and I suffered badly from home sickness. I'm not sure if there is an official illness that makes up home sickness and you will not know how bad it is, unless you have been affected by it. Irish people will be very familiar with it because of our heritage of emigration over many years. It is an aching in the heart and mind that pains you every day. You see people and things which remind you of home and it triggers it off again. At the same time, I would search for anything that would bring me closer to home. I would go to places where an Irish group might be playing music or even go to a pub that might have only one Irish record on its jukebox.

I suffered from home sickness for many years and, if I am honest, I think I still get pangs of it. That explains why as a family we would return home to Ireland every few months. I have spent a fortune in keeping my Irish roots alive. Over all these years though it has only served to alleviate the problem for a short period as it was worse than ever when it was time to return. It is a bigger problem for those people who emigrated to the United States, Australia and New Zealand, because of the distance. I feel so sorry when I see the many people who are having to leave Ireland now, as result of the recession, because I know what they will go through.

I was not over religious, but I did find great comfort in attending Mass on Sunday because it was an event that I was used to, and it provided me with a constant link to my earlier life. At stages over the years I did drop off from going to Sunday Mass for short periods. It wasn't that I was any less a believer. It was just that I was so busy and often working. These days, I have the luxury of having the time to be able to attend Mass regularly.

I do believe however that you do not have to be overly demonstrative in your love of God to be a good Christian. You can pray and communicate with God in your own private place. Very rarely a day would go by without me saying a prayer or thanking the Lord for looking after me and my family. I believe we all have a Guardian Angel to guide and protect us. I think my Guardian Angel looked after me well.

My initial six month contract had passed and I had stayed. There came a time after about two years when home sickness did get the better of me and I returned back to my old job in Ireland. I hadn't been back a week when I knew I had made a mistake. I could not settle in the small town again. So I went back to Yorkshire and continued where I had left off. My girlfriend from Castlecomer had now joined me in Yorkshire. I had been going out with Marion Ryan for over a year by that time, and we had kept in touch by writing when I went to Bradford.

Relationships between boys and girls were quite different from today, and there were also differences between lifestyles in Ireland

and England. Back in Castlecomer, for example, you had to have been going out together for a long time before you got to put your hand on a girl's knee. Many young ladies in Bradford were much freer with their affections. Contraception devices such as the pill and condom were not freely available in Ireland because of Church and legal restrictions whereas condoms were available to buy in the UK. I used to be hugely embarrassed to go into a chemist shop and ask for condoms. I would have a blushing red face and a stammer, so usually I would opt for buying the condoms from the vending machines in the pub toilets. When going back to Ireland on holidays, I would stuff my bag with condoms and be very popular with most of my friends who used to buy them from me. I'm sure most of them were never used, but it was a macho thing to have one in your pocket.

Adhering to our own culture, when Marion arrived in Bradford, she stayed in her own digs, while I stayed in mine. Our parents would not have been happy if we had started co-habiting. It wasn't until we were formally engaged and close to our wedding that we moved into a rented house together at 3 Steadman Terrace. This was Taz Singh's family house, but they had moved out and upgraded, so we rented it.

I had come back to Bradford after my brief return to Ireland. Although I was still feeling unsettled, I was now familiar with my surroundings and I was driving. I had passed my driving test after taking six driving lessons which made me very proud. Whilst I had driven in Ireland, it was a completely different matter in the UK because of the high-speed motorways and the volume of traffic.

My first car in Bradford was a Rover 3½ litre Saloon. It was a beautiful classic car with full leather interior (mind you, it was 10 years old). That set the scene for many years to come where I would buy large luxury cars that were more or less on their last legs and run them to the ground. I would pay cash down for those cheap cars and so, unlike my friends, I did not have any bank loans for my transport. It was only in my later life that I began to buy new modern cars.

Meanwhile, I was getting bored with working in Comer Yarns. Fred had left and I was now the factory foreman. I was also driving the company lorry and van and making deliveries all over Yorkshire and Lancashire. The textile business in Bradford and Ireland was going through a bad time, and I could see the writing was on the wall for Comer Yarns. So I decided to 'spread my wings' and head for a new life in London. At the back of my mind I still had visions of emigrating to the USA or Australia, but not just yet.

CHAPTER 4

LONDON CALLING

My older brother Joe was living in London with his wife, Teresa, and two small children Mandy and Caroline. The plan was that I would go to London and stay with Joe while checking out the job situation. Marion stayed in Bradford, but would join me later, if I settled.

I arrived at Joe's house in Tooting, South West London, on a Saturday morning. The following Monday morning I went out with Joe to look for a job. There were several pages of job advertisements in the local paper, but rather than replying to them, I decided I might get faster results by just going out and knocking on doors. I had no idea what type of job I was after; basically, the best job I could get. I had the confidence to try my hand at anything.

We visited three establishments that morning and I was offered three jobs to start immediately. Would that happen nowadays! My first job offer was in a small chemical works where I was offered a machine operator's role. The pay was quite good too. The second job offer was in a bookmaker's shop. I had asked the manager whilst Joe was putting a bet on a horse. My third and final offer that morning was at a firm called Fry's Diecasting Works, at Wembley. I was told the only job available was in the office, and I was asked if I was able to type and do filing. I exaggerated my previous experience of three days in the mining office, and I showed the excellent references I had got from Comer Yarns. I got the job. I went back to Joe's house to consider which job I would take. I decided the office job at Fry's would be better for my long-term future. And so, a few days later I turned up at Fry's in my clean white shirt and tie for my new career.

Fry's was a large foundry, producing items such as car engine components. There were hundreds of workers in the foundry and many dozens in the offices. My role was that of a progress chaser. It was my responsibility to ensure each order was processed as rapidly as possible to meet contractual deadlines. Basically, I was monitoring the number of items produced by checking counting meters on each machine. I counted how many items each operator manufactured and then converted the data to a bonus payment system into their wages. I settled quickly into my new job. Most of the foundry operatives were of African descent and I had a lot of trouble in spelling and pronouncing their names. I'm sure some of them received a bonus in their wage that should have gone to their colleague with a similar name. Equally, they had trouble in understanding my Irish accent. I spent most of the time in the large open plan office, but I also had to walk through the foundry several times a day. I sweltered in the heat of the foundry, but the Africans loved it. They would shout at me if I left the door open any longer than was necessary – "Hey, man, you're letting the cold in".

There were three tiers of management. I was on tier 3, the lower management level. The second level was those who had been there longer, and were more experienced. The first tier was the senior managers. They would not talk to my level or even look at us, if they could avoid it. They even had their own toilets which we were barred from using. I knew I was not going to stay in London too long, so I began to take some liberties at work. I would nip into the senior managers' bathroom rather than walking to my own. Each manager had their own individual towel with the name embroidered on it. I was drying my hands on one of them one day when a senior manager came in and caught me. He was a large man with a huge 'handlebars' moustache and a pompous accent. He gave me a right rollicking.

There was so many staff in the place I reckoned I would not be missed if I wasn't there. I took advantage of this and used to go home early every day. I was part of the management team which meant I did not have to sign in or clock in and out. On a Friday I would only work a couple of hours and then set off to Yorkshire to see Marion and my friends. I can't have been too important as I was never missed.

In London I got a flat overlooking Clapham Common. I always thought it was strange to look out onto the common on an evening to see men walking hand in hand. Strange place London, I thought. That wasn't my scene. I was at home in any of the hundreds of Irish pubs in London. So many Irish people and Irish music – it was like living in Ireland again. I thought there must be more Irish in London than there was left in Ireland.

I enjoyed living in London, but I couldn't see a long-term future there, so after a year I went back to Bradford. The economy was booming and I had the pick of dozens of jobs in Bradford. I did not want to return to the textile trade, I wanted to move on and do something different. I had been working as a part-time security officer with Securicor at Mount Street. My job had been to patrol various commercial premises in a van with an Alsatian guard dog.

I knew the people at Mount Street, and they knew me and I had no problem in getting a full-time job with them. I started as a static guard at commercial sites, but then graduated to become a cash-in-transit (CIT) officer. My job was to transport cash, sometimes millions of pounds, all over the country. I was part of a team of five senior cash-in-transit officers carrying cash between the cash centres situated in Yorkshire and the Midlands. One of my regular runs was to Birmingham and return, four times a week. We used to drive two heavily armoured vehicles, one was carrying cash and the other acting as a decoy to distract any would-be robbers. We knew we were often followed and watched by criminals, and on occasions, when acting on criminal intelligence, armed police officers would escort us.

We came to grief in the early hours of one morning on the A38 dual carriageway near Burton-on-Trent, as we made our way back towards Yorkshire. We were travelling at in excess of 70 mph when the rear axle on my van seized up. The van careered out of control and overturned several times. It went across the central road barrier and we ended up on the opposite carriageway. I vividly remember seeing a 32-tonne lorry driving in the opposite direction, bearing down on us, and managing to avoid us at the last moment…

The three of us in the van all remained conscious. My two colleagues managed to escape from the crashed van, but I was trapped and badly injured, hardly able to move. I smelt the fumes of petrol falling onto the hot exhaust and engine, and I feared the van was going to go on fire with me inside. I had several broken ribs, a broken pelvis and deep lacerations and could hardly move as I was in such pain. I thought I would surely die on that quiet dual carriageway unless I got out of the vehicle. My door was bolted and locked. The windows were made of thick bullet-proof glass and would not break. My only route of escape was through a small emergency exit hatch in the roof of the van. Somehow I managed to open the hatch and climb out to safety...

One million pounds in bank notes was left in the van guarded by police officers as myself and my two colleagues were taken to hospital. I was the most seriously injured of us all and had to stay in Burton-on-Trent hospital for several weeks. The company looked after me as well as they could, and they arranged for Marion to travel down to see me every day. After four weeks, I was moved to Bradford Royal Infirmary. That made it much more convenient for me to have visitors.

After three months sick leave I returned to work. The crashed van was in the yard at work as it was a total write-off. I couldn't believe how we managed to get out of it alive. My Guardian Angel was certainly looking after me that night. I settled back into work and soon afterwards I was promoted to be the assistant manager of the cash-in-transit services department. I had also left my weekend textile job when I had gone to London. Again, not wanting to return there, I went in a new direction and got a job as the assistant manager at the Odeon cinema in Bradford. This was a large striking, iconic building in the city centre. I wore a smart dress suit and a bow tie and was a general dogsbody to the manager. Best of all, I got to see all the films for free. I think I saw The Sound of Music and Clockwork Orange so many times, I knew the script off by heart.

At some stage about that time I had proposed marriage to Marion, and she had accepted. I say 'at some stage' because I can never remember doing it or just how it came about. We have always joked that she got me drunk and just made it up. As we were living together for a while, it was inevitable we would get married. We went to Ireland and we told our parents we were going to get married. They were fine about it. We had the option of a quiet wedding in Yorkshire, or a full-blown event in Castlecomer. It was a no-brainer really, and we went with our culture of the big Irish wedding. I was working hard and I could afford to pay for it. Everyone getting married will tell you of their problem in deciding who to invite. Our problem was worse because we had so many friends, and Marion's family is huge. "To heck with it" – I said – "just invite them all". And so on 26th of March 1976 we got married in the Church of the Immaculate Conception in Castlecomer followed by a big traditional wedding reception at a hotel in Carlow. We then had a week's honeymoon touring Ireland before returning to Yorkshire.

I was now a married man living and working in Bradford. In my mind I still harboured thoughts about going further afield to the USA or Australia. I had come to Bradford on a six-month contract, and I was still there three years later. I still had not settled in Bradford and I felt very homesick most of the time.

Chapter 5

The Police

In late 1978 I got the idea that it was time for a change in career again. I was aware the police service had just had their pay and conditions reviewed and improved. It looked an attractive time to join. More than anything I saw it as a challenge to get selected, and to get through the rigorous training programme. If I was good enough to get selected, I thought I would stay no longer than 12 months before emigrating again.

I responded to a newspaper advertisement and received back an application form. When I say 'a form', it was more like a book. It would be enough to put most applicants off, but I persevered. I detailed all my past jobs and gave examples of my experience in several areas of competencies. I also had to detail every small bit of my private life. I sent the application back with not a lot of confidence. I thought they would recruit their own rather than enlist an outsider. The Troubles in the north of Ireland had been at their worst for several years. Irish people in the UK were regarded with suspicion and in many cases there was open hostility to the Irish. It was not so many years earlier that you could read notices for jobs or accommodation stating NO IRISH / NO BLACKS. I spoke with a strong Irish accent and I was used to being looked at with some disdain and suspicion.

I was a bit surprised to get a reply sometime later to say I had progressed to the next stage. The second stage was to sit an entry examination. At the appointed time and date I went to the Tyrls Police Station in Bradford city centre where I was one of a group of about 20 young people sitting the exam. I was concerned that the sergeant who was overseeing the exam spoke to a number of the candidates and addressed them by their first names, as if they were old friends. All of my previous interviews in the UK had focused only on my knowledge and ability. Unlike in Ireland, the interviewers were not bothered about my religion, if I played sport or if my family were well off. I thought to myself, what chance have I got if the sergeant's friends are here for the job. However, I need not have worried. It transpired that a number of the applicants were regular attendees and had failed the exam on previous occasions. The exam was quite difficult, but, happily, there was no Irish language requirement, and a week later I was notified I had passed.

The next stage was a home visit by a senior officer to assess my suitability. An Inspector called to our house one evening and spoke to myself and Marion for a while. He was called Inspector Butterfield, and I was to get to know him very well over the coming years as he would be my team Inspector for a while. He was quite an extrovert man and a bit mad in his personality style. We must have had something in common as he passed me to the next stage, a medical and fitness test which I passed with flying colours. The final stage was to be a formal interview before a panel of three senior officers at Wakefield headquarters, but first I had to be vetted to ensure that I was a suitable person for the police force. Any black marks in my character or lifestyle – and that would be the end of it.

My background checks took a long time because of the enquiries having to be made in Ireland. They were getting references from my friends, employers and former teachers. They checked with the Gardaí that I had no previous convictions. My fine for not having a driving licence had not been recorded and did not count against me. I know my vetting procedure was far more rigorous than other candidates' because of my Irish background. Understandably, they would not want to employ anyone with republican or loyalist connections.

The interview at police headquarters was very demanding. It seemed to go on and on for an awful long time. Coming to the end of the grilling I wasn't too sure how it had gone. The chairman asked me finally – "Why should we appoint you above the other candidates?" My confidence came to the fore and I cheekily said – "Because I am better than them, and, if you give me the chance, I'll prove it to you". I believe that one sentence swung the interview in my favour as I was told soon afterwards that I had been successful. I was going to be a police officer. The whole process of getting employment had taken over a year and was the most difficult job process I had ever undergone.

On 5 October 1979, I made my way to the Bishopgarth Police Training Academy at Wakefield. I would be away from home for most of the next four months. The schedule was planned as one week local induction training at the Wakefield Academy. Then 12 weeks away at the regional police training centre in Dishforth, North Yorkshire. After that followed a further two weeks local training at Wakefield, before being posted to a division somewhere in West Yorkshire. Several further weekly courses would be taken over the course of the first two years, along with on the ground training at my designated police station. At the end of the two years' probation stage I would be either confirmed as a competent police officer, or have to undergo further training, or be dismissed, if not up to standard. I saw this as a challenge and I resolved to get through the training programme successfully.

West Yorkshire police then had a force of about 5000 police officers, supported by approximately 3000 civilian officers. It had responsibility for an area of 780 square miles and 2 1/4 million people with large busy city centres, towns, villages and quiet rural areas. An excellent network of motorways and trunk roads made it easily accessible for other UK populated areas. The population, whilst obviously being mainly Yorkshire English, was also rich and varied in its range of ethnic cultures and economic backgrounds. Three million calls for assistance were received from the public each year; that is, one call almost every 30 seconds. This volume of work did not take into account the self-generated incidents that officers would activate themselves whilst on patrol. Coming back to the training period, there was an intake of 16 recruits in my particular class. We were told we would get our posting when we returned from the district training centre after 12 weeks. We knew we could be posted anywhere in West Yorkshire, but we didn't know where. The only certainty was that it would not be in the area where we were living.

I stayed in the hostel at the Academy and I was well looked after. Three meals a day were supplied free of charge and a nice clean room with all facilities on hand. In that first week I was taken to the tailor supplies centre, where I was measured and kitted out with my new uniform. When I say 'measured', it wasn't exactly what you might expect. So long as the uniform fitted reasonably well, that was it. I passed down the store's conveyor belt with item after item being handed to me. I couldn't believe the amount of clothing and equipment I was given. Traditional police helmet, flat peaked cap for wearing in a car, the very best of overcoats, one for cold weather and one for rain. Leather belts, several trousers and tunics and numerous shirts. Baton and handcuffs and a multitude of other items filled my car boot. I thought then, this is great for protection from the weather, but I didn't know how I could ever run in all this gear.

I was also taken to the local Magistrates' court where I was officially sworn in as a police officer before a Justice of the Peace. I was given my warrant card with my photo on it, and I was now officially a police officer. In reality I didn't feel like a police officer – I still had so much to learn. The first few days had been comfortable enough. I was getting the feel of my new environment and making new acquaintances with my fellow classmates. The training officers were generally inspectors and sergeants and they all seemed decent, reasonable people. Things were going well, but that was all about to change…

By day three, we were all kitted out in our new uniforms and looking very smart. I'd had my hair cut short in a neat and tidy square back and sides before I came to the Academy. My new Doc Martens black shoes were highly polished, shiny and clean. We were introduced to the drill sergeant, Sgt Billy Barnes. He was a powerfully built man who stood upright as if someone had shoved a pole up his behind. He pushed his chest out like a pigeon going courting. He didn't speak to us in a normal voice, but instead shouted in a loud squeaking manner, so it was difficult to understand what he was saying, most of the time. His uniform was pristine, and his boots so highly polished that they looked like glass. He carried a drill stick which he tucked under his arm like the sergeant majors I had seen in the cartoon films. To reinforce everything he told us, he would periodically hit the desk in front of us as hard as he could with the stick. He gave us a quick inspection and took each of us to task over just about everything. He barked at me that my hair was too long and that my shoes and uniform was a disgrace. He told us how to iron our uniforms and gave us tips on how to put a perfect crease in the trousers and arms. By rubbing some dry soap inside the crease before ironing, it would stay sharp for much longer. He showed us how to polish our shoes to a high standard. He taught us the 'spit and polish' method. I would use a soft cloth to put a little polish on the shoe – it had to be the very best polish only. Then I had to spit onto the cloth and rub it with my fingers in small circular strokes for ages…

We were dismissed at 5pm to have tea and get ready for a full inspection and drill training the following morning. My first task after tea was to visit the barber. He was a Polish man who had set up a temporary barber's shop at the Academy. I explained to him, I would like a short trim and square at the back. He took no notice whatsoever and proceeded to cut all my hair off almost completely. There was no style or shape to it at all. In those days long hair was the fashion and it was rare to see such short hair; it certainly wasn't trendy.

I then spent hours pressing my uniform and brushing it until it was looking ever so smart. My ironing experience up to that had been limited to the odd shirt now and again. I then spent a couple of hours polishing my shoes until they were sparkling. An hour's revision of the day's laws lesson took me up to 11pm, and I was ready for bed. It had been a long day's work.

First thing the following morning we were ready to go on the parade square. As a class we were coming together as a team and helping each other. We checked each other's uniform for fluff and made sure our helmets were fitted properly. We first watched Sgt Barnes put the police cadets through their paces. He shouted and barked at them whilst they went through an impressive marching routine. They marched like a battalion of professional soldiers, although they were no more than young teenagers. I thought to myself, he's going to be disappointed if he thinks I can do that.

Soon it was our turn to line up. Sergeant Barnes instructed us on some basic marching and saluting moves. He used one of the cadets to demonstrate how it should be done. There was a brief moment of comedy as the cadet demonstrated how to stand to attention. He stood at ease in front of Sergeant Barnes. The sergeant shouted 'TENSHUN!' and the cadet stood to attention and stuck his chest out with such force that a button flew from his tunic and hit Sgt Barnes in the face. We fell about laughing, but the sergeant wasn't at all impressed. His face grew redder than a tomato and he screamed at the top of his voice that it was time for our formal inspection.

We stood to attention as the sergeant came down the line addressing each of us in turn. I was in the middle and he had bollocked everyone before he reached me. He told us that any discrepancies he found would be severely punished. The punishment would range from extra patrol duties in the evening to going to see the Academy commander for a verbal bashing, and we could also face a further disciplinary inspection the next morning.

He asked me where I was from and I said – "Ireland". Maybe I should have said 'Bradford', because he picked it up straight away. From that moment he only ever addressed me as 'Irish'. He then inspected me and touched my helmet forward with the stick, revealing what little hair I had left. He screamed at me that it was still too long and ordered me to have it cut again. He said he would check it the following morning.

Then he found a speck of fluff under the collar of my tunic and told me I was on disciplinary inspection the following morning for that as well. He looked at my highly polished shoes and barked at me – "These are disgraceful, Irish, get them done tonight and I will see you on the discipline parade for these as well in the morning". By now his face was so red and he was so excited that I thought he might have a heart attack.

And so that afternoon after tea, I was off again to see the Polish barber with another pound in my hand for another haircut – the third time I'd had my hair cut that week. I knew the sergeant and the barber were friends and I wondered to myself then if they were sharing the profits. Maybe a silly thought, but these visits were well over the top.

After the barber had mutilated the little bit of hair I had left, I went back to the hostel where I caught up with my fellow classmates. We spent the rest of the evening polishing our shoes and ironing our uniforms. I wasn't the only new officer to be on the discipline parade the next morning, but I was the only one to be there for three breaches. We had a good laugh about it that night, but even so I wasn't looking forward to it.

The next morning we went again to the drill square… The drill sergeant called "Hair!", and those of us with the 'hair problem' went forward for inspection. This time, my hair was 'all right'. It really had to be because I scarcely had any. My beloved locks fell victim to the Polish barber. Then he shouted "Uniform!", and I went forward again with a few others. He spent minutes inspecting me in detail before begrudgingly telling me that I still had 'to improve' on it. Then he barracked "Boots!", and I was off again. He said – "you again, Irish" and warned me to work harder on the shoes.

The remainder of my encounters with the drill sergeant over the first two years was to be on similar lines. He was never happy with anything I did. Of course he picked on many others as well, but he seemed to be consistently looking to find fault with me.

Of course, I can only speak about things as I saw them, and how they affected me. But I thought I was actually a very well-behaved student officer, I was respectful to everyone and I was extremely well turned out. I saw this drill sergeant as a bully who singled me out because I was Irish. But I knew I could not beat him, so I kept my nose clean, worked hard and kept out of his way as much as I could.

It is ironic that particular drill sergeant was highly regarded within West Yorkshire Police. No senior officers would hear a bad word said against him, probably because they were afraid of him, and even now he is regarded by many as an iconic figure of the force. I never had any respect for that drill sergeant and neither did a lot of my colleagues. I would only ever refer to him as the 'gobshite sergeant'.

Discipline is an important aspect of a police officer's work, and it is absolutely right that a great emphasis is placed on it. However, it can be instilled in people without belittling them or bullying them. There is also a danger that if training officers use bullying or intimidation that those same officers go into their communities and adopt the same behaviour when dealing with the public.

The first week at the local training centre came to an end. I now had some inkling of the task in front of me. I knew I had so much to learn. The drill sergeant had made my first week a misery, but I never for one moment ever thought about leaving. I was ready for a hard slog, so I shrugged my shoulders and carried on. I was on home leave on the Saturday and Sunday, but, once again, most of it was spent on revising lessons, pressing my uniform and polishing my shoes.

Chapter 6

Dishforth

On Sunday evening, I headed off on the 90 minute drive to the district training centre at Dishforth in North Yorkshire. This was an old RAF base and in a poor state of repair, but was still partly operational. The sound of fighter jets taking off and landing was commonplace and was often very disruptive to our learning. We couldn't hear the instructor talking and would often be distracted looking out the window at the jets.

There were a hundred trainee police officers on my course from all over the UK. We were housed in large dormitories with beds side by side and a small wardrobe each. Men and women were housed in different blocks and we were under pain of expulsion, should we be found crossing 'the borders'.

There were several classrooms, a large gymnasium and a social club also on site. There was a village with a small pub a mile away, but we were not allowed out of camp. Sometimes on an evening we would run across the fields to visit the pub, just to be daring and for a change. Coming back home again through the field meant we were covered in mud, and it wasn't really worth the effort. We used the social club on site to go for a few drinks on an evening. We would not go overboard because we knew we were being watched and assessed by the training staff all the time. In any event, after revising and getting our kit ready we had very little time for drinking.

Life at the training centre was very hard, both physically and mentally. We usually started at 7am with a shower and shave in cold water as we rarely had the luxury of hot water, and we would still be going at 9pm. Some mornings we were up at 4am to go cross-country running or swimming. I found the swimming tough as I wasn't a great swimmer. It was my least favourite subject and it was made worse by having to get up in the middle of the night to do it. The other students had the advantage of having learnt to swim at school, but there was no such thing as swimming lessons at the Boys National School in Castlecomer. The swimming lessons I had taken when I arrived in Bradford were now coming in useful. The life-saving techniques we had to pass were difficult – retrieving items from the bottom of a deep pool while fully clothed and dragging a heavy dummy body for long distances. However, I managed to reach the required standard.

Standards of dress and deportment were every bit as high as they had been at Wakefield. There was even more emphasis on marching, drilling techniques and saluting. We had to salute every officer of the rank of inspector and above. Sometimes that caused a bit of a problem recognising who to salute. I came to the conclusion that it was easier to salute anybody who was older than me and moved.

We were split into classes of about 15 students each. There was intense rivalry between each class generated by the class tutors. We studied all aspects of the law in depth. The law is very complex with so many points to prove for each offence and so many defences to overcome. A lawyer or solicitor will spend several years at college and university learning the law and still have the advantage of being able to reach for a reference book when in doubt. A police officer has to have an even better grasp of the law. He will have to make instant decisions and does not have the luxury to have instant access to a law reference journal.

We were allowed home on a Friday evening and had to be back again on Sunday evening, we had an exam first thing each Monday morning based on the previous week's subjects. If a certain mark was not reached, then extra lessons had to be squeezed in to rectify the deficiency. On every Monday morning, it was always interesting to see how many students had dropped out and not returned to camp. You could always bet on one or two resigning, particularly during the first month.

In those days there was a lot of anti-Irish feeling amongst the general public in the UK, caused in part by the situation in the North. It was also a time when political correctness had not yet arrived, and various racial jokes were commonplace, even on television programmes. As a result, I felt there was an added pressure on me to do well in everything I tried to do, The most common Irish joke revolved around the idea that the Irish were stupid. I believe that sometimes they were told in a mischievous manner and in a way that was intended to stir up anti-Irish hatred. I did not like these jokes and if someone told one in my company, I would let them know I did not like it.

I have to say that there were no obvious signs of such behavioural thinking at the police training centre, but I knew some people would still secretly subscribe to such views. In my time at the initial training stage and indeed throughout my entire police career this sentiment drove me to always work that bit extra harder, and to be better than everyone else. I still got an ear bashing every now and then for not having my bed made perfectly or for having a spot of dust under my wardrobe – the sergeants missed nothing. The difference at Dishforth was the trainers and instructors were decent people and not intimidating bullies. I learned a lot from them, and to this day I always make my bed properly when I get out of it and my bathroom towel is always neatly folded.

I also grasped the academic side of the course and was amongst the highest mark scorers in the weekly exams. As we neared the end of the 12 week course all of us students who had 'survived' had become close friends and bonded into a formidable unit. Over 30 years later that close friendship still exists in many cases.

We had a formal dinner and passing out parade at the end of the course where our families could attend. Marion came up to join me. During the formal presentations I was delighted to be awarded a plaque for being the joint top student of the course. As I collected it, I thought to myself – "Up yours to the 'thick Irish' jokes!"

The following Monday morning saw me back at Wakefield headquarters for a further two weeks local procedure course. Some of the stuff I had learnt at the district regional centre would be implemented differently in each police area, and I had to learn these changes. I also had the misfortune of renewing my acquaintance with Sgt Barnes again. He remembered me as 'PC Irish', but it was a far more confident PC O'Shea who paraded before him. He didn't frighten or intimidate me, although he tried. I just played him at his own game and said "Yes Sgt, no Sgt", while at the same time I was thinking to myself – "Feck you, Sgt gobshite".

On this course we had more time to ourselves on an evening and we used it to familiarise ourselves with the public houses of the town, followed by a kebab on the way back to the hostel. As a class we were now far more relaxed and confident in our own company. We had lost some members who had found the going tough and resigned, but those of us who had survived so far were having a good time. We didn't go mad with our socialising as none of us were too flush with cash. I had actually taken a substantial pay cut to join the police and I was also now a married man. At that time I was driving a large old Rover car and it was costing me a fortune in running costs.

It was on this course that I learnt where I was to be posted. I was going to be stationed at Odsal division in Bradford South. That was on the other side of the city to where I was living, but I was happy with my posting as it wasn't going to be too far to travel and I already had a basic knowledge of the layout of the area.

CHAPTER 7

THE REAL WORLD

After my two week course at Wakefield I had been given a week's leave. Now, on the following Monday I had turned up for my first shift in the real world of policing. I was on the 2pm to 10pm evening shift. I was on my own as all the other new officers had been posted to different stations throughout the force area. Odsal police station sat on the top of a roundabout, overlooking the famous Odsal stadium. It was a large, imposing old building, but it was also dark and grim-looking. Not surprisingly, it has since been demolished.

I found my way to the parade room where the afternoon team were preparing for their tour of duty. Next door the morning early turn team were being debriefed before going off duty. My team was team four. It was comprised of about 20 constables, three sergeants and one inspector. I was told to just observe proceedings until they had time to deal with me. The parade actually took place at 10 to 2 because the team needed to be ready to go at 2pm.

As it got nearer the time, everyone busied themselves brushing their uniforms and shoes, making sure they looked their best. Then the sergeants shouted "Parade!" as the inspector came into the room. Everyone stood to attention holding their batons and handcuffs out to the front to show they had all the basics to perform their duty. I recognised the Inspector as Mr Butterfield, the officer who came to visit me when I applied to join the force.

The Inspector quickly checked each officer in a light-hearted and casual manner and advised one or two on minor issues such as hair length or shoe cleaning. Then one of the sergeants briefed the team on several items of interest that had taken place during the previous 24 hour period. He also briefed them on persons who were wanted and other items of interest. There then followed a particularly large section relating to the Yorkshire Ripper. The officers were briefed on the current state of the investigation and things to look out for whilst they were on patrol. Then each officer was told what their duties were for the day. All were given a particular beat to cover and told if they were on foot patrol or driving a vehicle. There were also told when to take their meal break.

It struck me there was an awful lot of information to absorb in a short space of time. However, the team obviously knew what they were doing as the whole thing was concluded in a quick and efficient manner. Whilst discipline was maintained throughout the meeting, it was conducted in a far more relaxed manner than I had experienced at training school. After the briefing the officers set off on their designated tasks. Sgt Anton took me under his wing to show me around and explain how they worked.

The overall responsibility for the team rested with the team inspector. The day-to-day management was performed by the sergeants. One sergeant acted as station sergeant, dealing with matters at the station. The second sergeant looked after the clerical aspect of the team, checking the files the officers submitted and allocating enquiries to them for investigation. The third sergeant – referred to as the patrol sergeant – supervised patrols and incidents outside in the division.

Six patrol cars covered the division supplemented by two traffic cars, a public order van and a dog patrol unit. It was a large division, mainly covering the south side of the city. It was a totally built-up area containing several large local authority housing estates, private housing estates, large shopping centres and commercial areas. As a police officer, it is necessary to know your division intimately both geographically and by knowing the diverse communities living in it. This would be one of my priorities.

I would work in company with a tutor police officer for the first couple of months until I was deemed competent enough to work on my own. I met PC Keith Pickles who was to be my tutor. He was an experienced police patrol officer getting towards the back end of his career. Keith was a gentleman who had an in-depth knowledge of police patrol work. He was also blessed with the patience to be able to work with a complete novice like myself. His task was to allow me to gain as much experience in different areas of policing as possible. Unlike the other patrol officers who were sent from one job to another, Keith was able to pick and choose jobs so that it best suited my overall training.

That first day I was issued with a locker, a radio and everything else I would need. My pockets were stuffed with items and I had everything but a kitchen sink attached to my belt. The first job we attended was a road traffic accident where a car and a motorcycle had collided. The motorcycle rider was injured and had to be taken to hospital by ambulance. We measured the scene and got the vehicles moved off the road, so traffic could move again. Then we took details from witnesses and went to the hospital to check on the condition of the injured party. Luckily he was not badly injured. Then back to the station where we submitted a written traffic file report.

This was far more exciting than the training school, although I was concerned at the amount of time we had to spend at the station doing reports. That particular trend did not alter a lot in all my police service. So much time has to be spent doing clerical, filling forms and submitting reports. Probably the most significant change over the years was that we moved from paper to computer files.

By the end of the first shift, I was pretty much punch-drunk with too much information. At 10pm we all gathered for the shift debrief. The sergeants checked what issues we had dealt with and how we had resolved them. Then we were dismissed. I learned then that it was very much customary to go to a local friendly hostelry for a few wind down drinks. If you didn't go with the group, then you could be regarded as a bit of an outsider or oddball, and this could make life difficult. It posed no problem for me to socialise after work as I was a bit of a social animal. This was also a great way to get to know each other and have a laugh and a joke. We never got much time to speak at work, we were so busy. Drink-driving was an issue which we were very careful about as we prosecuted people for it. We certainly couldn't be seen to do it ourselves, so we were very careful about the amount of alcohol we drank.

At this time my wife Marion and myself were living in a rented house at Leeds Road in Bradford. Marion was pregnant and we were keen to upgrade to a better standard of accommodation. One of the perks in joining the police was you could qualify to live in a police house. I received a fairly generous rent allowance in my pay, but I could relinquish the allowance and get a house provided instead. I opted to do this and I looked at a number of police owned houses that were available. I chose a nice three bedroomed semi at Broadway Close off Manchester Road. It was in good general condition and had a large garden. It was certainly an improvement to where we had been living. My local shopkeeper, Mr Patel, had a large white van and he allowed me to borrow it to move our stuff to the new house.

Most of the other houses in our small cul-de-sac were also occupied by police officers and we quickly made new friends with our neighbours. The police maintained the house in a good state of repair for us and even sent someone to cut the grass every now and again.

As it happened, one of the sergeants on my team lived across the road from me. Sgt Bill White was a lovely man who was nearing retirement. He worked as the station sergeant, dealing with matters within the station and supervising our control room. I got to know Bill and his family very well and he gave lots of advice to me as a young officer. Some of my other neighbours worked in different police stations and departments and by talking to them I was able to get a broader view of the force. This helped me to make more informed decisions later on in my career as I moved around the force.

In those days we worked a 3x8 hour shift rota system – 6x2 days, 2x10 evenings and 10x6 nights. Punctuality was a big deal. It was a serious matter to be late for parade and anyone falling foul of this rule was guaranteed a telling off by one of the supervisors. One of my colleagues told me he had been late for duty once in 15 years. He was 10 minutes late because of a puncture on his cycle. There was no mercy – he got reprimanded and fined for being late.

In the middle of the shift we were allowed a 45 minute meal break. It was rare, however, that we would get a full uninterrupted 45 minute break. Calls from the public to West Yorkshire police for assistance were coming in at a rate of about one every 30 seconds. Our breaks were staggered so as to maintain cover and a lot of the calls were graded to appointments, but still emergency calls requiring an immediate response would almost always lead to us interrupting our meal and dashing out to another job. The sergeants understood this and, when it was quiet on the odd occasion, we would be allowed to stretch our break to 1 hour. We usually played cards at meal times. We played bridge for a small wager, but nobody ever won as it would invariably end in a draw. As the new recruit from training school, I was still one of the smartest officers on the team. It wasn't expected that the established patrol officers would have shiny high polished boots or creases in their uniforms. After all, this was the real world and there was little time to be worrying about such things. The type of work we did meant we could be covered in mud chasing a suspect or rolling around on the ground trying to arrest someone. Our shirts too, would often be covered in blood and, more often than not, it would be our own blood.

I began to settle in to the routine of police patrol work. I had not had my police driving course yet so I wasn't allowed to drive a patrol car. I was either on foot patrol or doubled up in a patrol vehicle with an experienced officer. On other occasions, I was given internal jobs such as working in the control room or acting as a gaoler to the prisoners.

I spent several weeks with Keith, my tutor constable, and he did his best to get me as much experience as he could. I ticked off a list of jobs to be done, such as sudden deaths, road accidents, robberies, burglaries, assaults, shoplifters, missing from home enquiries and other general welfare checks. Keith was great and took his time in showing me what to do. As my confidence grew though, I began to be impatient and I wanted to move a lot faster. Other younger officers on my team were getting to deal with far more exciting incidents than myself and I felt I was missing out.

At one of my regular appraisal meetings the sergeant recognised I was doing well and suggested I should move up a gear and work with some of the younger, more dynamic officers. To some extent it was a case of running before I could walk properly, but it was exactly what I needed and what I wanted at that particular stage. I knew all of the officers on my team by now and they were all different in their own way. Some were quiet, some were loud, some were timid and others tended to be more physical. Most were enthusiastic and hard-working, volunteering for jobs and seeking out their own self-generated work. A few were downright lazy and would dodge work by spending as long as possible on any menial task. On occasions we would be speeding to the scene of a violent incident as a result of a 999 call only to spot one of the lazy officers driving in the opposite direction. They would have the piss taken out of them in the briefing room at the end of the shift, but it didn't seem to bother them. They were thick-skinned.

From day one I had been surprised at how busy we were kept and the type of work we dealt with. The radio operator was constantly in our ear sending us to jobs. More often than not, all the officer units would be engaged and the operator would be shouting for a unit to attend an emergency call. We would respond by leaving our routine call, hoping to return later when finished with the emergency call. Through no fault of our own sometimes we would not get back to the routine call. This caused bad feeling with the first caller because their routine call was very important to them. However, we were so busy we had to prioritise.

Many of the calls we had to deal with were mundane, time-consuming and a good percentage of them were not even jobs for the police. Poor supervision in the call centre led to us running around when the callers should have been re-directed somewhere else in the first place. We had regular callers for some strange incidents. One person regularly called us to deal with a ghost in the house. Another – because the birds were chirping too loudly outside his window… Others would tell of dreaming about serious crimes. I didn't know what I was expected to do about it. Then there was the endless list of neighbour disputes. Each neighbour was as bad as the other. I just wanted to knock their heads together, but of course I couldn't do that. People would lock themselves out of their cars and their homes. I didn't have a skeleton key. My magic key was my baton, which I used to break the window with, but they could have done it themselves.

Calls from social services were a regular occurrence – 'please make a welfare check on an old person because the social worker can't be bothered to go today'. These checks took a long time as I couldn't just run in and out of an old person's home. I would make them a cup of tea and sometimes even go to the shop for them. Hospital welfare calls also took time. 'Please go see Mrs so-and-so and tell her, her mother is in Ward so-and-so. Can she come and see her and bring her a clean nightie'. In those days no one had mobile phones and Facebook wasn't there yet, so it fell to the police to pick up the pieces.

On top of these calls we had reports of burglaries, robberies, shoplifting, assaults, missing from homes, and road accidents. We had calls of people trapped in fires and really serious crime scenes, such as rapes, murders, shootings and kidnappings. Some incidents were complicated and made more serious because firearms had been used. In the early stage of my career firearm incidents were rare, but as the years rolled on, they became commonplace. We had to respond to the change and we adapted new procedures to deal with them. You cannot just send a police officer to knock on the door of someone armed with a gun. It has to be a properly planned firearm response with the safety of the officer, the public and the suspect paramount.

It was a similar case with regards to drugs in the early 80s. A few people were dabbling in cannabis, but it wasn't the massive problem that it is today. Nowadays cannabis has been overtaken by much harder, more expensive drugs that cause death and misery to many folk. It also brings financial riches to the top dealers and this makes it a cut throat business where extreme violence is often used to protect their assets. I often said, if it wasn't for drugs and alcohol, we in the police would have little to do.

Chapter 8

My New Tutor

My first shift with my new tutor, Constable Tom McDougal, was on a Monday night. We started duty at 10pm and worked until 6am for seven consecutive nights. We were accompanied by officer Russ Ablard and the three of us were designated to patrol in a police Ford transit van. Tom and Russ were both tough, experienced officers and they didn't suffer fools gladly. If they advised you to go on your way, it was a good idea to listen to them. They were not exactly politically correct training officers, but more in the style of combat operational officers which is what I felt I needed to develop at that time. With three of us on board we dealt mainly with public order incidents. Hence the van was commonly known as the Black Maria or Paddy's taxi.

The Irish had a bit of a reputation for fighting at closing time, but that was a bit unfair because just about everyone had a good fight when the pubs closed in those days and there weren't so many Irish in Bradford. Since then things have improved with regard to violence in pubs and clubs; obviously, some of the new measures have worked.

On the briefing before we started patrol there was an item about one of our local criminals who was using a newly acquired motor car. He was suspected of using the vehicle to travel to commit crime and also had no driving documents such as a licence, insurance or MOT. The man was well-known to officers at our station and amongst many others, was soon to be well-known to me.

I have always had an uncanny knack of dropping across people or things that made my arrest record look impressive. Some people saw it as luck, but in fact you actually make your own luck. It was down to me having a photographic memory for faces and briefing items and for being observant.

That Monday night was no exception, and as we drove around the Wibsey area, I spotted the villain's car driving towards us. I shouted to Tom and he turned our van around and followed the suspect's car. Tom managed to catch up with the car and I switched on our 'blues and twos' to tell the driver to stop. Immediately, we knew that he had no intention of stopping for us as he started driving away at high speed. Although we had the blue lights and siren on, our van was cumbersome and we had great difficulty in keeping up with the villain.

This was my first real chase of any length and it was very exciting. Very dangerous too, but Tom was an experienced advanced trained driver and he did exceptionally well to keep up with the car and at the same time, drive us safely. Still refusing to stop, the suspect's car drove on the wrong side of the road, went through several sets of traffic lights at red and narrowly missed other cars and road users.

After several minutes of such reckless driving he abandoned the car and made off running. Myself and Russ were straight after him and after a short chase managed to rugby tackle him and bring him down. Normally, when Russ put you down, you stayed down. The suspect still wasn't done and he fought violently with us, trying to escape, but we got the handcuffs on and arrested him. It was my first 'proper' arrest which had involved good observations, an exciting car chase and a violent struggle. I was well pleased with my performance.

Myself and Tom interviewed the suspect, but he wouldn't talk to us or answer any of our questions. In fact, he spat at us. My adrenalin was really pumping and I wanted 'to throw the book' at this man. We discussed the appropriate charges and we decided to charge him with driving without the relevant documents and resist arrest. With regard to the manner of his driving, Tom wanted to charge him with a relatively minor offence of driving without due care and attention. However, my shackles were up and I said he had committed the far more serious offence of reckless driving.

Tom said it would be far easier and less work for us to charge him with the lesser offence. I was adamant though that we throw the book at him and charge him with the most serious offence. That was a lesson I wouldn't forget. The basic rule in policing is – the more serious the charge you make, the more difficult it is to prove. The bigger the charge, the bigger the file, and ten times more work for the officer in the case.

A 'due care' charge would mean a small file taking about four hours to complete. My 'reckless' file was colossal and it took me about six weeks to see the back of it. The file kept coming back to me to include more evidence, road descriptions, conditions, weather situation, street lighting, speed limits, witnesses and drawings, photographs, etc etc etc. I was never much keen in dealing with road accidents and traffic files after that.

Mind you, I still think police officers should not be influenced by the amount of work involved. If it takes hard work to get a villain put away, then so be it. My hard work did eventually pay off when the driver received a custodial sentence and was banned from driving for a lengthy period. Not that he was the type to take any notice of the court ban, as I was to lock him up several more times in the future for similar offences. Our paths crossed again several years later for a final time when, as a senior detective, I worked on a murder case where he was the victim. It transpired he had upset someone because of his romantic activities and it ended with him being murdered.

Many of the families I had dealings with as a young copper, I was still dealing with them 30 years later. If I wasn't dealing with the same people, I was dealing with their offspring. Sometimes I thought – what chance in life do these kids have when you see how their parents behave. The answer, of course, is 'no chance at all', but it wasn't my problem to worry about that. I just locked them up, and, if they went back to their old ways, then that was their problem.

I remember one large family. I knew all of them by name, and could even remember their birthdays as I had locked them up so often. Every shift we would be called to one of their homes as they all lived in the same street. They would fight and rob from each other and expect me to sort it out. The next day they would be all friends again. They liked me and respected me because I treated them fairly and I got on well with them. I would see the old man going home drunk and I would say to him – "Behave yourself now or I will be around in an hour to arrest you". I just knew he would start trouble soon after arriving home drunk. I got to know the youngest son in the family quite well and I had hopes he would turn out differently.

Sadly, not to be, as many years later as a senior detective I got called out to another serious incident in the middle of the night. The names and addresses of the parties involved rang a distant bell in the back of my mind. At the crime scene I saw a body

I recognised as an older member of that same family. He had been stabbed to death. A few hours later, the young boy who I had hoped would do well, now an adult man, was exposed as the suspect. I traced him to a nearby address. He remembered me from his younger, happier years as I arrested him for the murder of the family member. I suppose it was inevitable that it would end like that.

Chapter 9

The Yorkshire Ripper

One of the sergeant's would brief us before we commenced our shift and went out on patrol. Various things would be covered, including wanted persons and areas of trouble requiring special attention. In early 1980 there was always one topic of interest that featured at every briefing – the Yorkshire Ripper. The North East of England and particularly the Bradford and Leeds areas were living in the grip of fear of a serial killer who had already attacked 14 women, killing 11 of them in the most brutal manner, and was still on the loose. The national press ran stories of the Ripper's activities and it was a topic of conversation everywhere you went in Yorkshire.

West Yorkshire police were conducting the largest murder investigation ever undertaken in the UK. The chief constable had been taunted by a man claiming to be the Ripper, who had sent him a tape in which he boasted he would never be caught. The voice on the tape spoke in a north east England, Geordie accent.

No woman felt safe walking the streets after dark. It was a black shadow over the whole of the north of England. I was far too inexperienced to be part of the Ripper enquiry team, but it still affected my everyday working life. So many officers had been drafted into the murder squad, it meant those of us left behind had to pick up the pieces and deal with their everyday workload as well as our own.

The daily briefing updated us on how the enquiry was progressing and what we should be looking out for on patrol. We were instructed to check the welfare of all lone women we came across on a night. That meant stopping and warning them of the dangers of being out alone after dark. Often we would convey the woman to wherever she was going to get her off the street and out of the Ripper's way.

We were also instructed to stop and check all males who were on their own especially those who might be acting suspiciously. An awful lot of men fell into this category. Of course, after the Ripper tape had been received we were mostly concentrating on men who spoke with a Geordie accent. We now know this tape was in fact a hoax, made by a man who had nothing to do with the Ripper. In years to come he was tracked down and sent to prison for a very long time for perverting the course of justice.

Me and my colleagues on patrol knew the Ripper was active in our area and we fancied our chances of being the one to arrest him and get our names into the crime history books. Every night after parade myself, Russ, Tom and our fellow patrol officers would get out on the street as fast as we could and start looking for the Yorkshire Ripper. We each had our own ideas of who he might be and we kept an eye on men we considered as oddballs or suspicious in some way. It became a competition amongst us to be the officer to catch the Ripper. In 1980, the Ripper struck again, killing two more women.

The Yorkshire Ripper was finally arrested in January 1981 after being stopped and checked by an ordinary uniform patrol officer in Sheffield. He was unmasked as a man called Peter Sutcliffe and he lived in Bradford – just a few miles from where I worked. The sheer size of the murder investigation had hampered the murder squad and allowed the Ripper to avoid arrest for too long. In the course of the enquiry he had been seen by the police on a number of occasions, but there was not enough evidence to arrest him.

In July 1979 he had been interviewed by a young detective called Andy Laptew, who had highlighted him as a good suspect, but the report was filed because Sutcliffe did not have a Geordie accent. I later became a friend and work colleague of Andy's. If only the hoaxer had not made that prank misleading tape, the Ripper would probably have been arrested earlier and some lives saved. In the Ripper enquiry days, of course, there was no computers. All the evidence had to be examined, indexed, cross referenced and filed manually. In an enquiry of that scale it was easy to miss clues and opportunities.

West Yorkshire police learned from that enquiry and soon afterwards all major enquiries were investigated using the computerised HOLMES system – Home Office Large Major Enquiry System. Since then computers have been used successfully in all major investigations. The difference it makes is truly remarkable.

The focus was on the Yorkshire Ripper murders, but other serious crimes were still taking place. In March 1981 the dangers we faced as police officers was highlighted when one of the sergeants at my station was murdered whilst on duty. I knew the victim – Sgt Michael Hawcroft – as a fine sergeant and supervisor. In the middle of the night he had disturbed a youth stealing a car. He tried to arrest the young man, but the youth stabbed him with a knife and killed him.

When I arrived at work at 6am that morning, a dark cloud of depression hung over the police station, yet everyone carried on with their job in a professional manner. The suspect had been arrested and was in custody. My job that morning was to act as a constant supervision officer to the prisoner. I stayed with him wherever he went and watched everything he did, in order that he could not harm himself. Even when he went to the toilet, I went with him – I watched him every second of the day. Justice took its course eventually, and the killer went to jail for a long time. I used to see the sergeant's widow and young children at our Christmas parties over the coming years. I always felt sorry for them that they had lost their husband and father and I knew that any sentence the court had given would not bring him back to them. The young killer would eventually be released, but they would never get over their sad loss.

I was doing very well at work. My appraisals were very good and I had no real issues or problems I couldn't deal with. That's not to say I wasn't finding it hard learning my way and gaining experience in the police world. Some things were a big culture shock to me. Most people I came into contact with would either lie to me or refuse to speak with me by abiding with their legal right to remain silent. I had been a naïve, trusting young man before joining the police, but now I was learning never to really accept anything I was told. This is something that has stayed with me throughout all of my career, and has served me well.

Not only did a lot of people tell me lies, but a large number of them wanted to fight with me. When I was being brought up in rural Ireland, we always had great respect for the Gardaí. We would speak to them with respect and certainly never assault them. I found many people I had dealings with in West Yorkshire had little or no respect for any authority. It was common for suspects to resist arrest and put up a fight, often injuring the police officer in the process. The difference as I saw it was due to the fact that in Ireland, you would be sent to prison for assaulting a Garda officer, whereas in the UK they were only given a slap on the wrist.

I never accepted that type of behaviour from anyone, and I would not allow anyone to get away with insulting or assaulting me. Where I came from, if you insulted or spat at someone, you found yourself on the floor stemming the blood from your nose, but my police training now kicked in. I had a quiet, polite and controlled temperament, but when push came to shove, I could defend myself – and had to do so on countless occasions. I often remember going home from duty with blood covering my uniform, although at home I would always play down the violent aspect, so as not to worry my family.

Chapter 10

On My Own

After six weeks patrolling in company with a tutor I was deemed competent to go on independent patrol. I was allocated my patch as Beat 6. This was the area of Marshfields, Little Horton and Canterbury estate. It was a busy built-up area of private- and local authority-owned housing. It had schools, pubs, clubs, shopping centres, factories and busy roads.

I remember my first day of patrolling on my own. I was on afternoon shift. I set off walking down Manchester Road. As I walked past shop windows I glanced at my reflection and thought how smart I looked in my full uniform, I hardly recognised myself. Manchester Road was comprised of a six-lane carriageway with three busy lanes of traffic going in each direction. There was a 3 foot high metal barrier separating the carriageways. As I walked down the road it was busy with school children just finished school for the day. The road had underground subways for pedestrians to cross safely, but many people just jumped over the barrier and dodged the traffic.

I saw a woman with a young boy of about six years old crossing the road. She got to the central crash barrier and lifted the child over the barrier and told him to stand there while she climbed over. As she climbed over the barrier, the boy ran across the road and was hit by a passing car. I saw the accident happen and it didn't take me long to get to the scene. Traffic had come to a halt and frustrated motorists were blowing their horns, obviously unaware that a child had been injured. A large group of parents and children had gathered around and some of them were upset and crying. They all looked at me and said – "The police are here. It's okay". I thought to myself – "Oh shit, I wish the police would come", but then I realised I was the police and I had to sort it out. To the public I was the police. They had no idea and were not interested that I had only been in the job for five minutes.

The child was not badly injured and I managed to comfort him and place him in the recovery position. I needed an ambulance and I needed police backup to help me with the traffic movement. To my horror, I was in a radio black spot and could not transmit. I had to marshal some help from some of the public bystanders to look after the injured child while I went up the road a bit to get a radio signal. Eventually I managed to get the boy to hospital and got the traffic moving again. I had learnt that although some people will be quick to criticise and disrespect the police, in their time of need they will always rely on the police to help them. Their expectations of the police are high at all times. They see a police officer and are not interested in how much or how little experience that officer has.

It's fair to say that the most difficult part of my patch was the Canterbury estate area and I spent an awful lot of my time on the estate. Domestic and neighbour disputes, fighting and general crime was rife. Cars were left on the streets with no road tax and no insurance. Many of them were vandalised and would end up as a pile of scrap on the roadside. I decided I would clean the area up and have a positive effect on the quality of life of the local residents. I made some enquiries as to who owned the untaxed cars and I served them with notices to remove them. If they were not removed, I arranged to have them taken away and scrapped. Packs of dogs were roaming the estate and again I made checks on the owners. I prosecuted many of them for having no dog licences and I forced them to take control of their animals. Many of the dogs were dangerous and I had them seized by the dog warden.

Soon the estate was a better place to live and I was appreciated by many of the residents. It is important to remember that the majority of the residents were decent, law-abiding people who had felt trapped in their own homes. I am glad to say that my presence made life a little better for them. Many of the residents trusted me enough to tell me who the troublemakers on the estate were. I had to sort it out on my own from that point because they did not have the confidence in the criminal justice system to go to court as witnesses. Who could blame them, they had to live there. I could only help them within the constraints of the law, though.

One woman called me to her home one day and complained that her 20 year old son had kicked her in the stomach and was regularly assaulting her. The son was in the house at the time. She told me she did not want her son to be arrested or prosecuted, but asked if I would take him in the kitchen and, in her own words, "beat the shite out of him". I explained that I could not do that, while at the same time seeing the pain she was in and thinking I wish I could beat the sod up. However, I decided to arrest him anyway and try to get enough evidence to prosecute him.

While I tried to restrain this young man, he kicked me violently in the groin. It really hurt, and as he came at me a second time, I gave him my best punch to the head, causing him to fall like a rag doll to their ground. He was used to punching his mother and it gave him a shock to punch someone who hit him back. I then arrested him, but I was unable to prosecute him for assaulting his mother as she would not agree to prosecute him and I had insufficient evidence without her. I didn't charge him with assaulting me either, as he had come off worse than me. It was still a successful conclusion. The mother was delighted that the lad had got his just rewards and the lad himself had no complaints either. I think he had learnt a lesson. He and his mother had immense respect for me after that and I was never called to deal with any more trouble from the young man.

Health and safety issues were not such a high priority in the early 1980s. I was often placed in an uncomfortable position that nowadays would be subject of risk assessments and perhaps dealt with much differently. One night a coach driver stopped at Odsal police station. He said he had 36 drunken men on board who had been to a stag party. They were vandalising his coach, fighting, swearing and drinking and making it unsafe for him to drive the coach. The sergeant who was on duty wasn't highly regarded by us for his effectiveness and that night he lived up – or down – to his reputation.

He took me to the coach with him, and when the drunken men saw the uniforms, it was like waving a red flag to a bull. They went berserk, calling us names and making rude gestures at us. They refused to quieten down, no matter how many times we asked. At that point the sergeant should have called for reinforcements and arrested the ringleaders, but he did not, he bottled out. He had the idea of getting them away from our division and delivering the problem to someone else. He instructed me to go with the driver on the coach until he got to Leeds and then bail out.

The nervous driver got on board and set off for Leeds with me as his escort. The sergeant went back to drinking his coffee while I was left to deal with 36 drunken thugs on my own. We hadn't got very far when I was showered with spit, cans of beer and parts of the coach seats. Some of the thugs were baying for my blood and I felt very intimidated and frightened for my own safety. "Bugger your daft idea, Sergeant" – I thought – "I have a better idea". I instructed the driver to take the coach to the Bridewell police station at Bradford city centre, where prisoners were detained and interviewed. Using my radio, I arranged for several other units, including dog units, to meet me there. When we got to the Bridewell, I shouted at the top of my voice that they were all under arrest. I got a barrage of further abuse which included some opinions as to my Irish parentage, but when they saw the police dogs and my reinforcements, they all became fairly quiet. You can just imagine what a queue of 36 drunken men looked like waiting to be booked into custody.

The Bridewell custody staff were known throughout the force as the laziest department. They liked to watch TV and play cards while the rest of us worked our socks off. They would moan like hell when they were asked to fetch a prisoner out of their cell for interview or to open a cell door. I was the most unpopular person in the world when I turned up with 36 prisoners to be processed. They had to be fully recorded, searched, fingerprinted, photographed and cells had to be prepared for them. I don't know if the Bridewell team on duty that night ever forgave me for ruining their tour of duty. The coach driver was happy though and thanked me several times.

The 36 men weren't really criminals at all. They had just got blind drunk and were behaving with a wild pack mentality. When they eventually sobered up the next day, they were very embarrassed and even apologised to me. All 36 of them appeared at Bradford Magistrates Court on public order charges and were found guilty and given some minor punishment. They wouldn't all fit in the court dock and had to spread right across the public seating area in the courtroom. To this day, I believe I still hold the record for having the most prisoners at any one time in the dock at Bradford Magistrates Court.

The case was so unusual, it attracted quite a bit of media attention and I received a lot of positive feedback for my work. I also received my very first commendation as a police officer from the chairman of the Magistrates for what he described as 'bravery and effectiveness in dealing with a very difficult situation'.

The superintendent's policy in my division was that all officers would patrol alone, but we liked to work in pairs for health and safety reasons. We worked more effectively and had more confidence in dangerous situations when we worked as a pair. We also shared the paperwork which gave us more time on the streets.

The sergeant would give us our patrol instructions at the briefing, and would then check on us during our tour of duty to ensure we were patrolling on our own and in our designated area. Of course, once we got 500 yards from the station, we would join up with our partner and patrol together. When the sergeant would call on the radio for our position to check us, we would quickly split up. The sergeant would then visit us and give us 'a chalk'. 'A chalk' simply meant that a supervisory check had been made and an entry would be made in our official pocketbooks to that effect. That worked fine, but sometimes we would meet the sergeant, quite by accident, and he would see that we were double-crewed. This would result in a 'red chalk' when the sergeant wrote a warning in red ink in our pocketbooks and also gave us a reprimand.

One evening myself and my partner Dave Kirk had one such rollicking from Sergeant Anton who had found us double-crewed in Kirky's patrol car. There wasn't a lot we could say, we just accepted the rollicking and went our separate ways. We were still fuming about being told off an hour later and had crewed up again together when we heard a code 10/13 call come over the radio. A 10/13 call is an emergency call from another officer saying they are in trouble and require immediate assistance. It does not matter what you are doing when such a call goes out, you drop everything and go to the aid of your colleague. A code 10/13 would bring dozens and dozens of police officers from all over the city to your aid in a matter of minutes. The sky would be blue with all the flashing lights.

This code 10/13 was from Sergeant Anton who was being attacked by two men near to where we were. Myself and Kirky got there very quickly to see the sergeant on the ground and two men attacking him. He had disturbed them having burgled a house nearby. Myself and Kirky ran at the men and a very violent struggle took place. One of the men had a large spanner in his hand and, in order to disarm him, I aimed a hefty kung fu style kick at his arm. Unfortunately, I missed and instead kicked Sergeant Anton with some force on the thigh making him grimace in pain. We eventually managed to overpower the two men and they were taken away. Sergeant Anton nursed his painful thigh and said that was his worst injury. Half in jest, he suggested that I had kicked him on purpose for telling me off about double-crewing earlier. Of course, it was a total accident. But it did show the sergeant the dangers of solo patrolling and the benefit of having two officers come to his aid so quickly. Still, he was only enforcing the policy of the superintendent, who was sitting safely in his office drinking coffee. I vowed, if I ever got to a position of management, I would deploy my troops more effectively.

CHAPTER 11

THE COURTROOM

I still had to learn fast. I was regularly going back to the training academy to attend many courses and extend my knowledge of police work. The training schedule was very thorough. Amongst the courses I attended and passed successfully were first aid, policing techniques and complex law courses for serious crime. Although I had a driving licence and drove my own car, I was not allowed to drive police vehicles until I underwent a police driving course and passed a specific police driving test. I attended a three week advanced police driving course. You don't realise how little you know about driving until you've been on one of these. I was taught how to drive at high speed safely and I spent long hours simulating ice and snow conditions on the skid pan circuit.

Being in a busy city division meant it wasn't difficult to build on my experience with the vast range of incidents I had to deal with. I also spent some time on attachment to a large psychiatric hospital learning about the needs of the mentally ill and how best to deal with them. I attended courts on a number of occasions as an observer. First I went to the Magistrates Court. It was a fairly new complex in the city centre. There was nothing too grand about the place, it looked like it had been fitted out by MFI and I wasn't overly impressed. A procession of defendants came in and out of the dock. It seemed no one actually got dealt with, everything getting adjourned to a later date.

In those days it took ages to get the simplest of cases finalised at court and it was easy to see why. The defence solicitors made application after application for adjournments on the flimsiest of excuses. They used every trick in the book to screw more money out of the legal aid system and, ultimately, out of the taxpayers' pockets. It took many years for the penny to drop and the government took steps to restrict the legal aid cash cow by not allowing frivolous adjournments and so speeding up the whole process.

I also spent some time observing proceedings at the Crown Court. Bradford Crown Court was then part of the town hall building. The place was steeped in history and had an air of formal elegance about it. The judge sat on his bench high above everyone else wearing his gown and daunting wig. When passing sentence, you almost expected him to don a black cap and sentence the defendant to death. There was not as much time wasting in the Crown Court. The judges were professionals whilst the magistrates were volunteers – and it showed.

Many of the defendants at court were not bothered by the whole charade. They were used to it, and viewed it as an occupational hazard to get caught now and again. For many police officers, on the other hand, it was a stressful experience to give evidence at court. I have given evidence in court on hundreds of occasions. The seriousness of the cases ranged from the most minor offences such as shoplifting to the most serious, such as murder. I have given evidence in Magistrates courts, Juvenile courts and Coroners courts. I have been to the highest courts in the UK, including the Old Bailey and the Criminal Courts of Justice in London.

In every case there is pressure on the officer in the case to get it right and get a conviction. In the more serious cases, the pressure is colossal. The victim's family are depending on you to get them justice and the eyes of the nation are watching through the press reporters and TV teams. There is nothing that can relatively compare to the atmosphere created in a highly charged murder courtroom atmosphere – especially when you are concerned with the case under trial. The usually controlled hostility between the opposing factions is apparent for all to see. The intense drama unfolded by crucial witnesses as they enter the witness box heightens the anxiety of the victims' family and friends. The apprehension, the suspense and the tension explodes in a cascade of emotions when, finally, the jury spokesperson delivers the verdict to a hushed courtroom.

Courtrooms can be very cold, unfriendly places to be. I came to the conclusion that the courts were never too concerned as to whether the defendant in the dock had actually done the dirty deed he was charged with. The whole case would revolve around whether I had done my job properly and within the guidelines of the law. The law can be complex and these smart-ass lawyers are adept at finding loopholes. More often than not their defence would not deal with the question of the innocence of the defendant, but would attack the credibility of the police officer or other witnesses. If they could find the police officer has left any weakness in the prosecution case or transgressed the rules of gathering evidence, then their client would usually walk free.

It is one thing to have your case examined in detail for mistakes and rightly so, but in my experience it's a completely different thing to be accused of being corrupt. This is the second line of defence for the lawyer when the first has failed. Whenever I stood in the witness box and the lawyer accused me of fitting up his client, I would smile as I knew he was now losing the case and clutching at straws. Why on earth would I jeopardise my own reputation and indeed my freedom, to frame someone who I scarcely knew? If I thought they weren't guilty, I wouldn't bring them to court in the first place. Sadly, the courtroom is still an arena where games are played out. The result is often to the detriment of the justice system and to those who want justice to be done. The criminal justice system weighs heavily in favour of the criminal and the defence lawyers who know how to manipulate it to their own advantage. A huge amount of work and commitment goes into every successful conviction at court. With the odds stacked against us I think the police do exceptionally well.

In the future I would like to see a major overhaul of the criminal justice system to take into account the wishes, welfare and feelings of the victims of crime. Only lip service is paid to it now. Granted, there have been some improvements over the years, but nowhere near enough. It sometimes sickened me to see how a young thug who had broken into an old woman's house, assaulted her and stolen her property was treated in comparison to the victim.

After being taken into custody, the thug complained of feeling unwell. A doctor was summoned and attended almost immediately. An examination revealed nothing untoward, but an attention-seeking distraction and a successful attempt to waste some of the time that the police were allowed to question him. Then time is spent in getting an appropriate adult to sit with the young thug so that he is not intimidated by the police. His parents can't be bothered to attend, so Social Services are contacted to send a social worker to sit with him. Although the young thug can deal with everyday living in the UK, he now discloses whilst in police custody that he does not understand English and requests an interpreter to assist him. The nearest interpreter is 100 miles away, he will jump on a train and make his way to Bradford. He may well have to stay overnight in a hotel, if the interviews drag on – which it undoubtedly will, all at the taxpayers' expense.

The thug is also entitled to the free services of a solicitor which he duly requests. Free to him, but not to the taxpayer. The officer in the case must now coordinate the arrival of the social worker, the interpreter and the solicitor so that the thug can be interviewed. Just as the interview is about to begin and all the parties are present, the thug complains he is feeling unwell again and requests a doctor. The interview is put on hold and a doctor is again summoned. This time the thug reveals he is a heroin addict and is suffering 'cold turkey' from lack of the drug. The doctor prescribes him some methadone, heroin substitute, and declares he is unfit to be interviewed and must have 8 hours of uninterrupted rest. So be it, we will convene again in 8 hours' time and try to progress the investigation. In the meantime the prisoners' clock is still running – getting closer to the point when he will have to be charged or released.

In contrast, a detective has spent one hour taking a written statement from the frail old victim. She is not physically injured, but is frightened and vulnerable. Her stolen pension book and bank card needs to be cancelled and replaced, but she is too confused and upset to be able to deal with it. Her door lock is broken and a joiner will need to fix it. She doesn't know a joiner and she doesn't know if she can afford to employ one. The officer cannot spare any more time to help her. He must now try to contact a relative or a friend who will look after the victim.

As the case progresses to court over the course of the next few months, the same scenario is replayed time and time again. The thug is cosseted and looked after while the victim is very much left to fend for themselves. Victim Support Services do their best to support and assist victims, but they themselves are not financed or staffed enough to provide the many demands of support that victims need. The vast majority of the Victim Support staff are volunteers who willingly give their time and experience to help others for no financial reward. In my view, they should be properly resourced and paid a decent wage.

Another important example of putting the criminal aspect before the needs of the victims happens a lot in homicide cases. It is common for a victim's body to be kept for weeks or even months to facilitate the wishes of a criminal suspect. A suspect may wish to have the body retained for further forensic examination for his defence case. Where no person has been charged in connection with the death, it is also common to retain the body for lengthy periods just in case a future defendant may wish to have it forensically examined. This is terribly distressing for the family of the victim who want to hold a funeral and allow their loved one to rest in peace.

This problem could be resolved easily enough if the authorities were of a mind to ease the pressure on the victim's family. A forensic pathologist always performs an examination on behalf of the police and prosecution case. After that has taken place, instead of retaining the body for the benefit of the defence, an independent forensic post mortem examination should take place and the result made available to the defence. The body could then be released to the family at a far earlier stage.

It's high time the Government should get the priorities right and make the welfare of crime victims more important than the welfare of the criminals.

CHAPTER 12

FAMILY FIRST

In June 1980 a tremendous development took place in my life when my first son, Craig, was born. I took some time off from my busy work schedule to help Marion at home. We made arrangements for Craig to be baptised and, of course, like all our other family events, it had to be performed at our church in Castlecomer in Ireland.

We were regular visitors back and forth to Ireland, keeping in touch with our families and friends. Usually we would fly with Aer Lingus from Leeds Bradford airport or Manchester. Flying was expensive in those days, and it would cost a weeks' wage to fly to Dublin, not like today's budget airlines. In those days we used to dress up to fly as it was a bit of a posh thing to do. Once we got to Dublin, I would rent a car and travel down the countryside.

In September 1981 the process was repeated when my second son Darragh was born. Money was now getting tight and I was working a lot of overtime to keep my head above the water. With a wife and two children my dream of emigrating further afield was now becoming a distant dream, but that did not bother me as I was perfectly happy with my life. The delight of having children surpassed anything I had ever achieved and, although I loved my job, it was now relegated to second place in my life.

In those early days of my police career the troubles in the north of Ireland were very serious. Serious incidents were taking place in the Republic too. Police officers were being killed regularly and I was well aware that, although I was a member of the UK mainland force, I could still be a target. As a police officer I was advised not to travel to Ireland, but if I did, I should take sensible precautions. There was no way I was going to stop from going home, but I did my best to keep safe. My family was well known and respected in our town and I didn't expect anyone to cause us trouble. But you just can never be sure in those circumstances; it just takes one misguided idiot.

I would inspect my car underneath for booby traps every time I used it. We had a licensed shot- gun in the house and I would sleep with it beside my bed every night. I got one or two frights when there was banging on our front door in the middle of the night, but it was only some of the neighbours wanting to use our telephone to call a doctor for a sick child. I asked my mother not to broadcast it to everyone that I was in the police. She was proud of me though, and she still told everyone. I went in pubs and clubs where the IRA were actively supported and never had any trouble. Over the years I've made these trips hundreds of times without any incidents. I have always been accepted as being one of the locals, although working and supporting my family in the UK.

CHAPTER 13

BARNEY RUBBLE

Having successfully completed my police driving course I now was a regular patrol car driver. I would usually drive any of the many police cars, and sometimes I drove the public order van when I was on public order patrol. I didn't have much patience with troublemakers and neither did most of my colleagues. When called to a street or pub disturbance, I would open the rear door of the van and say to the drunken fighters – "It's your choice, go home now or get in the back of the van". More often than not the message got through to them and they dispersed.

It was much harder being a driver as opposed to a foot patrol officer because I got sent to far more incidents and I covered more ground. On foot patrol, I would have my favourite 'tea spots' where I would get a rest and pass some time away. I didn't get any time for drinking tea as a driver, but it was much more exciting to be a patrol driver and the extra work did not bother me.

The superintendent in charge of the division at that time was known by the nickname of Barney Rubble. He looked like one of the Flintstones' characters. He was a strict disciplinarian and would find fault with everything, never recognising any of the good work done. It was always the best policy to keep out of his way. He had a habit of inspecting the patrol cars when they were parked up between shifts. If he found them untidy or dirty, he would find out who had used the vehicle last and then suspend their driving permit for up to a month, depending on the gravity of the 'offence'. His system was flawed because he didn't always identify the driver correctly. He called me to his office one day and said he had found a cigarette end and cigarette ash in my car. I have never smoked in my life so I knew I wasn't responsible and I protested my innocence. Nevertheless, he suspended me from driving police cars for 1 week. I wasn't too bothered as I fancied a rest anyway, and I would get one while on foot patrol. He had actually found fault with most of the patrol cars on that particular day, and this caused a massive problem on the following day. At the briefing, the sergeant was frustrated to find he had no patrol drivers as we had all been suspended by the superintendent. The superintendent has just given no thought to the impact his daft policy would have on the practical issue of policing the area.

Another episode when he demonstrated a total lack of common sense also involved me. I had been feeling ill for several weeks with a bad abdominal pain. It would come and go every few days. I was on duty one day when the pain hit me with some force and I collapsed. I was taken to hospital where they diagnosed a burst appendix. My system was poisoned and I was in a lot of discomfort. After a few days I was recovering in hospital after my operation when I had some visitors from the station. The superintendent – Barney Rubble – was accompanied by one of the officers in charge of our social club. The social club officer gave me flowers, fruit and a 'get well' card from my colleagues. Barney Rubble handed me a brown envelope. In my naivety I felt sure there would be a cheque in it to cheer me up and help me financially and I felt bad because I had always previously regarded Barney as a plonker.

I opened the envelope and I was very disappointed to find a notice of complaint with my name on it. Some member of the public who had been arrested in a mass brawl had made a complaint against all of the officers that had attended the incident, me being one of them. Barney said to me – "I had this on my desk to serve on you". To actually come to see me in hospital when I was quite poorly and serve me with a discipline notice was disgusting. It could easily have waited until I had returned to work and again it demonstrated the lack of sensitivity of the man.

On the subject of complaints, it is always accepted by officers that people will make complaints about the police. A police officer is not a politician and cannot go around smiling and agreeing with everyone, promising them the world. We have to be the people who enforce the law, we say NO to people, we move them on, we arrest people and we prosecute them. We have to defend ourselves and within the constraints of the law we have to be violent to some people. Some people object to this and they will make complaints. It is right and proper that they should be able to do so, and any officer found to be guilty of an infringement should be punished appropriately. I am certain though that the more work a police officer does, the higher the rate will be the complaints against them. In all my career, however, I have never had one complaint against me upheld.

Make no mistake that complaints against the police are fully investigated. I would even venture to say they are more thoroughly dealt with than any run of the mill crime reported by a member of the public. The Independent Police Complaints Commission (IPCC) and the Crown Prosecution Service (CPS) seem to like nothing better than to prosecute a police officer.

Back on duty after my operation, and I was soon as busy as ever. There was a certain amount of excitement around and much adrenalin flowing when I drove through the city at speed with my blue lights and siren sounding. It wasn't easy finding my way around, but there was no time to stop and look at a map and we did not have satnav in those days. By repetitive patrolling I learnt even where the most remote and obscure roads and avenues were.

One fun way we developed our local knowledge was by playing hide-and-seek in the police cars. If it was quiet in the middle of the night one of us would hide in our police car by parking up in a difficult place to find and where we would not be seen so easily. The other patrol cars would go searching and the one finding the 'hider' was the winner. It may sound as if we were wasting time, but that wasn't the case at all. This was a very effective way for us to learn our way around the city and would enable us to get to an emergency call in double quick time. It also had the effect of getting patrol officers into areas where they would otherwise rarely ever be seen.

Another seemingly daft idea we had was to conduct patrols while driving backwards. Let me explain. There was a general fuel shortage which seemed to go on forever. Like everyone else, the police had difficulty in filling up, and so our commander issued a new daft policy – we were ordered not to exceed 20 miles per shift in order to save petrol. Keeping under 20 miles in an eight hour shift was almost impossible. It meant we had to park up and only drive to attend emergencies. General patrolling was more or less stopped completely.

Then we had the bright idea that in the middle of the night, when there was very little traffic about, we would patrol the housing estates whilst reversing in the patrol car. If we exceeded the 20 mile limit, we would reverse until we were again below the limit. It still used fuel, but at least we were performing our function and patrolling our division. I don't know what the locals thought when they saw us going down their street backwards, maybe it made some of them give up the drink.

CHAPTER 14

MY GUARDIAN ANGEL

I was beginning to get used to violence by now and, unfortunately, I was often the subject of that violence. Amongst other things, I had a bottle thrown at me when I was on duty at Leeds United's Elland Road ground. I managed to dodge the bottle, but not the snooker ball that followed it. To add insult to injury, I was actually a Leeds United fan at that time! A muscle-bound bouncer took exception to my search warrant one day and landed his 22 inch colour television on my chest. A vice madam also took exception to my search warrant one morning and attacked my face with her long 'scissorhands' fingernails. My trusty colleague Geordie Davison was too busy laughing to come to my aid.

In those early days I was armed to the teeth with a wooden police baton. That was it, no CS gas, no firearm and no body armour – not even a bloody whistle! I never resorted to using my baton a lot, only on just a few occasions. At 2am one morning I stopped a car with three men in it in Halifax Road as they were acting suspiciously near a garage forecourt. When I flashed them, the driver got out and came towards me, leaving the two passengers in his car. I knew he was trying to divert my attention away from the car and so I took him back to examine it.

The passengers got out and I then spotted several car radio/cassette players in the back. They had been visiting forecourts stealing from parked cars. Before I could say or do anything, I felt an almighty bang to the back of my head, where one of the men had hit me with a club of some type. The blow knocked me to the ground and then all three of them set about kicking and punching me. I had no chance against the three of them, I just rolled up in a ball to minimise the damage. Then they got back into the car and began to drive away. I was up in a flash after them, but there was little I could do to stop them. In some frustration I drew my baton and I smashed the driver's window. The car still moved away and in a final rage I threw my baton at the rear window, causing the glass to shatter. The last I saw of the car was it disappearing out of sight with my baton sticking out of the rear window. It did have the desired effect though, and made it easier for my colleagues from CID, Crime Investigation Department, to track down the car and arrest the men.

I was also required to use my baton on a number of occasions in what turned out to be a frequent scenario. There was a large psychiatric hospital in our area. Every now and then some of the patients would get violent and we would be called. One of the most violent patients was a man called Pete. His little episodes were always the same. He would assault the staff or some of the other patients and then proceed to smash the place up. He would place himself at the top of a wide staircase and await our arrival. The sight of uniformed police officers made him far worse and, as we climbed the stairs, he would repel us by kicking out or throwing furniture at us. It was a dangerous situation, but we got used to dealing with him in a way that none of us got injured.

Two or three of us would rush up the stairs, one of us with our baton drawn. When we got to him, if I was the one with the baton, I would hit him as hard as I could across the shinbone, which is very painful, but would not cause any serious or lasting injury. This would momentarily distract him while we grabbed him and struggled to get handcuffs on him. He was such a big strong man that he frequently broke the handcuffs. The nurse would appear then and sedate him with an injection. After that he was Mr Nice Guy for another week or two.

One night I was on my own driving through a red light area in a neighbouring division when I was stopped by a prostitute who told me a man had been hanging around her looking very suspicious and threatening. Prostitutes live in a twilight type world where irrational behaviour is commonplace. For her to report it to me indicated she was frightened and concerned. She gave me a description and I had a drive around the area to see if I could locate him. It was about 1am in the morning and the area was quiet. I was in a built-up industrial area with no residential houses and not very many people about. I spotted a man scurrying down the street. As I got closer to him, he quickly turned down another street, seemingly trying to avoid me and all the time keeping his face turned away from my police car.

I stopped the car just ahead of him and quickly got out of the car to speak with him. "What are you doing here, lad?" He never answered, but quickly and purposefully moved towards me. He drew his hand up to shoulder level and I could see he was armed with a long thin-bladed knife. I could now see his face and there was no mistaking the evil intent in his wide open eyes. He never said a word, but made a quick slashing movement with the knife that connected with my chest area. Then he ran away. Luckily, it was a slashing movement rather than a forward thrusting attack, otherwise it would have been far more serious. It was a warm night and I was only in shirt sleeves. The knife ripped my shirt and drew a little blood from my chest. I made the decision not to chase him, I knew he would not hesitate to kill me, if I gave him the chance. As I was out of my own division and on a different radio frequency, it took a little longer than normal to get backup to me by which time the knifeman was long gone. I'd had a lucky escape, and I'm convinced someone was looking after me that night, like my Guardian Angel.

I was getting very efficient and adept in dealing with an increasingly high number of police type incidents. However, the occasions where violence had been directed towards me, told me loudly and clearly that my personal safety was at risk. I needed to wise up significantly in that department, or I wouldn't survive too long. I learnt this can be achieved through experience and training and I made it a priority to learn – and learn fast. I would never turn my back on someone who could be a threat to me. I watched their body language and listened to what they said. I took account of the tone of their voice because it can tell you a great deal. I would search them for weapons, and in cases where I perceived a threat, I would forcibly restrain them and handcuff them. When I conveyed a prisoner in a police car, I would never allow the prisoner to sit behind the driver for fear of throttling the driver and causing the vehicle to go out of control. Whenever possible, I would call for backup from other officers to support me in tricky situations. I'm sure my adherence to these basic health and safety precautions helped me survive a dangerous career.

In the coming years the force realised officers required more protection and our training in self-defence tactics was much improved. We trained very regularly with weapons and hand to hand combat. The equipment available to us was much improved, too. We were issued with modern batons that were far more effective and stronger handcuffs that were quicker and easier to apply. More of us were armed either with lethal firearms or electronic Taser guns and we all carried CS gas. We also had our own personal protection stab and bullet-proof armoured vest and other protective clothing.

Soon after my stabbing experience another incident came my way that gave me the opportunity to show that I was learning fast. It was one of those rare evenings when I was on foot patrol in a quiet, dark street in the Wibsey area. I noticed a young man acting suspiciously. He was wearing a jacket with the collar turned up and a woolly hat that concealed all but small part of his face. He walked up and down by some houses looking at the windows. The curtains were drawn, but it was possible to see inside through some of the gaps in them. I thought he was either a 'peeping Tom' or was looking for a house to break into. I got close to him and I shouted – "Let's have a word with you, what are you doing here?" He mumbled – "Nothing", but he looked really uncomfortable and agitated. He said – "I'm going home. I live up there", pointing up the road. Maybe I had misjudged the situation and got it all wrong. Maybe I was going to look very silly. In that moment though the strangest feeling came over me. I felt a distinct coldness come over me as if I had walked into a butcher's freezer. Something was not right and I could sense a form of evil near me. Acting very quickly on my instinct I thought – "Here it goes, it's shit or bust" and I lunged forward at the lad and pinned him to the wall. He resisted me and I saw he was struggling with something in his right hand. I grabbed his wrist and felt the blade of a knife. He had the knife handle held in his hand, and the blade was concealed under his jacket sleeve. The blade was so long, he wasn't able to get it out with one hand. I managed to get his arm up his back and I disarmed him.

It was indeed a frightening looking knife and again I had had a lucky escape. The youth was called Robert and he was 19 years old. He had some mental health issues, but was not considered serious enough to be sectioned. When I interviewed him in the presence of a psychiatric social worker, I didn't get much change out of him. I wasn't able to ascertain why he was carrying the knife or what he was up to when I had apprehended him. I charged him and he went to court. I don't know what penalty he received, but it wouldn't have been a great deal. I realised that Robert posed a real threat and after I finished dealing with him, I submitted an intelligence report about him. In the report I highlighted that he was a very dangerous man and I predicted he would kill someone. My supervisor vetting the report thought I had gone a bit over the top and was exaggerating. It seemed a bit presumptuous for someone of my limited experience to make such a statement. I was proved right less than a year later though, when Robert killed another youth in another part of the city. He was then detained in a secure unit for life.

This was the first time I had experienced a cold sensation that warned me of an evil presence, but it wasn't to be the last. Over the future years it would warn me of similar instances where evil was present or had been present. I wasn't over religious, but I did believe I had a Guardian Angel looking after me and I vowed to listen to it in future.

I had no close-up experience of death or how people were affected by death before I joined the police service. I just never knew death was so common and the regularity of it all. I was now dealing with death on an almost daily basis. While it was part of my job, I never became immune from the grief and sadness it brought with it. I was hardened to it, but I was still also very sensitive to the effects it brought on others. I always found it most difficult dealing with child deaths, probably because I was a family man myself, and knew what it meant to have children. I would come home from duty and the first thing I would do was to hug my kids and thank the Lord for looking after them.

As a patrol officer most of the deaths I dealt with were sudden deaths of elderly people. Most of the cases were straightforward and would be certified by a doctor as natural causes. Other deaths, where younger people were involved and could not be explained, was a different matter. I treated every death as a possible murder scene. I would preserve the scene and gather evidence until the CID experts came and took over.

It was a similar scenario with road accidents and industrial deaths. Whereas I would deal with run of the mill accidents, all the senior experts would appear and take over when a fatal accident took place or when the death was deemed to be of a suspicious nature. Sometimes my involvement would be to carry out death warnings on behalf of another police force. Can you imagine what it's like to have to knock on the door of a complete stranger and tell them that their loved one has died… I was counselled and trained in how to do it, but it was never easy. It would often spoil my whole day as I thought about it.

People react to such bad news in different ways. Some remain quiet and others panic and scream in anguish. We were advised not to get dragged into the grief by physically consoling the person, but I often did. Sometimes I would hold them and hug them, giving them a shoulder to cry on. It might not have been too professional, but it's the most natural thing in the world to do. Some death warnings took maybe 20 to 30 minutes until relatives or friends rallied around. On other occasions, where the person was on their own, I would stay for as long as was necessary, making cups of tea, consoling them, and advising them of the procedure that would take place. All the time the radio operator would be in my ear looking to send me to another job.

This is an example of how different police work is to any other job. The pen pushers and time in motion study experts would allow five minutes to do a death warning. After all, it could easily be done in that time. They would not allow for the empathy, care and compassion that is needed at such a time.

In the years to come, as I progressed up the ranks in the police, death would become a far more integral part of my job and I would be the one making the crucial decisions of whether it was caused by natural causes or foul play. I would be the one with the stressful and dangerous job of finding the person responsible and convicting them at court.

CHAPTER 15

AUTO THEFT UNIT

I was now almost at the end of my two year probationary period. This is where a decision would be taken by my senior management whether to appoint me or dispense with my services. It was a no-brainer really, as I had been doing really well in the force. I had been amongst the top scorers in every exam and I passed all of my courses. My practical ability in day-to-day policing was also first class. I went to see the new superintendent – Barney Rubble had transferred – and he shook my hand and said – "Well done, welcome to the madhouse". I had now achieved what I had set out to do. I had managed to get recruited into the police and I had flown through a very demanding two year training programme. I was now getting itchy feet again and looking for a new challenge.

There are many different departments within the police force and this creates opportunities for staff to diversify. There are so many different options available, one should never be bored. In over 30 years I never let the grass grow under my feet and I moved on when I felt it was time to do so. This attitude, of course, makes life very difficult and stressful. Some people get used to a particular job and they stay there for their whole career. In that situation life is comfortable, they do the job almost without thinking too hard or using their brain too much. They know the best route to work, where to park and they know everyone they come into contact with.

In my career I moved about quite a bit. I tend to get bored easily, but it wasn't solely for that reason I moved. I wanted the experience of working in different areas and in different aspects of policing. I wanted to gain promotion too, but, most of all, I just wanted to test myself with a new challenge. It was never easy to begin again in a new environment. I often cursed my decision to move as I drove to a new place of work in the early morning. Finding my way there, finding where to park, messing about with new permits and passes to open security doors. Finding my way around the building and getting to know and remember the names of my new colleagues. That was even before I began to get to grips with my new role. You have to be able to hit the ground running in the police service. You don't get any sympathy from colleagues, and certainly not from criminals. The attitude is – you applied for it – now get on with it.

If you have a particular problem, you need to identify that problem through a problem profile and deal with it. You may try to resolve it amongst dealing with other things, but that will not be very effective. If you concentrate on that particular individual problem and dedicate your resources to it, you will get far more successful results. The police tended to work like that. Burglary, for example, was a huge problem, so a dedicated team of officers was set up to deal with it. They dealt with nothing else, and they were very successful. The crime rate for burglary offences was reduced to a much lower level.

One of the biggest negative impact areas on our crime figures was auto related crime. Stealing cars and stealing things from cars was a big problem. A team of police officers based at Manchester Road police station dealt with all the motor vehicle-related crimes in the division. Called the ATU – Auto Theft Unit – it was made up of two sergeants and 20 constables. It was rare for anyone to get into the unit until they had at least five years' service, but I managed to join even before I had fully completed my two year probationary period.

The Auto Theft Unit showed me a completely new way to police. No more uniform or marked police cars. We worked in jeans and T-shirts and we thought we were the Bradford equivalent of Starsky and Hutch. We only dealt with 'twocers' and TFMVs. The terms referred to the legal definition of the offences. Word 'twocer' originates from the acronym TWOC, taking [a motor vehicle] without the owner's consent, and TFMV means 'theft from motor vehicle'.

Although in plainclothes, we still worked to the letter of the law. We carried our batons and handcuffs out of sight. We carried police radios, but, unlike the patrol officers, the radio was no longer our master. We were not being sent from job to job. The vast majority of our work was self-generated. So, basically, you were as busy as you wanted to be. However, if you were not producing the goods, you would soon be on your way out. The two sergeants in the unit were fantastic. They motivated us, they pointed us in the right direction and still gave us the freedom to express ourselves. I learned a lot from the sergeants and I think the ATU experience drove my career in the direction of crime investigation.

Car thieves and those who steal from cars tend to be absolutely prolific. One active car thieve could take four cars a night, joyriding in them, dumping them and doing the same again and again. The same person could break into 20 cars in one night, taking the car stereos and selling them for cash. Multiply these numbers by about 20 active criminals and you can see the extent of the problem. When we arrested a suspect and used our interview skills to get them to co-operate with us, they would regularly admit to hundreds of offences. Most of these would be taken into consideration (TIC) by the court when sentencing was done. To some of these people it was like a drug or an addiction. They just could not stop taking cars and breaking into them.

Sometimes we adopted the 'wing and prayer' tactics. If the suspect had been out of prison for a few months and not been arrested, we would go and interview him on the weakest of evidence and often come away with him admitting to dozens of crimes. Some of these types were proud of their achievements in offending so often. Many of them saw it as a game between us and them and the occasional six months in prison would not deter them from their thrill. Often they would cruise around a police station in a stolen car goading us to chase them. They knew we often would not enter into a chase because of the danger to the public. It didn't make much difference as we would recognise them and kick their doors down the next morning.

Our crime numbers would often take a battering when there was a popular event drawing crowds and cars to our area. The streets around the Odsal Stadium and the Richard Dunne Sports Centre presented a golden opportunity to the car thieves when there were rugby matches, speedway races and stock car racing taking place. Despite our best efforts, dozens of motorists would return to find their car had either been stolen or broken into. We knew most of the offenders, so we adopted a disruptive tactic on an event's day. We would sit outside the suspect's house and when they went out we went with them. We didn't hide, we let them know that we were watching them. If the car thief went to the corner shop for cigarettes, we went one step behind him. We went everywhere they went. It was labour-intensive and some would argue it breached their civil rights of privacy, but it was also very effective as drivers would return from the stadium and find their cars were safe and well. The public wouldn't have been aware of the effort we had made to keep their property safe.

Whilst some of these 'twocers' regarded the whole thing as a game, it wasn't a bit funny if you were the one whose car was smashed up or had property stolen. The term of joyriding is not quite appropriate as sometimes the stolen cars were involved in serious crashes involving fatalities to members of the public and also to the twocers themselves. Even to have your car broken into is a massive inconvenience and an unsettling experience. The band Smokie came from Bradford and I remember one occasion when one of the members had his car attacked outside his house. Some expensive and essential musical instruments were stolen. Worse still, the band toured Europe a lot, so the musician's wife was staying at home alone.

She was very frightened by the incident, thinking the thieves could return again. Myself and my partner investigated this crime and we managed to identify four local teenagers as the culprits. We searched their homes and we recovered the stolen musical instruments. Our sergeant was delighted with our work, and as he was actually a big Smokie fan, he seized the opportunity to go meet his hero. We went along as well, to return the stolen items. The musician and his wife were over the moon when we assured her the youths would not be returning. It was as if a huge burden of anxiety been lifted. The sergeant was in his element, meeting his hero and having a tour of his studio. Myself and my partner were a bit surprised though, as the sergeant gave a blow by blow account of how HE had tracked down the villains and brought them to justice. The privilege of rank, I suppose. His nickname of Sgt Blagger seemed just about right.

The ATU was a complete success in managing the division's auto-related crime. The crime figures were kept very low and our detection rate was high. I played a major part in that success and it got me noticed. The unit was regarded as a training ground for future detectives. Like in any other job or profession, there is huge pressure on police officers to produce the goods and give real 'value for money'.

Almost all of our activities are closely monitored and counted. Supervisors are grilled each month by the senior management team about their officers' performance data figures. Comparisons are made in relation to the number of arrests, the number of court files produced, search warrants executed, persons stopped and searched. It is not possible to cheat on the performance system by using minor offences to increase numbers because the seriousness and gravity of the performance indicator is also assessed. It's quite right that it should be taken into account as for example a minor traffic offence might take 30 minutes to complete, a shoplifting

– four hours, but a serious wounding might take three weeks to resolve.

One day I got a call to go see the Detective Chief Inspector (DCI). He told me he was very impressed with me and that I should apply to join the CID as I would make a good detective. I decided the Crime Investigation Department was my way forward. Although I had the backing of the DCI, it was still a very competitive process to be selected. I was still very young in service to be going into the department. Other applicants were far more experienced than me. Still, I duly filled in the 30 pages of application, was granted an interview and was selected to join the CID. While I waited to join the CID I got a call one morning to return to the station and see the duty sergeant. He told me I was one of a number of other officers who was being sent urgently to the north Yorkshire police area to hunt for an armed police killer. Within 30 minutes I was in a van with 10 other officers heading for the Malton/Harrogate area.

Barry Prudom was a violent criminal who was on the loose in rural North Yorkshire. He had shot and killed an unarmed police constable in cold blood. A week later he had shot and killed an innocent civilian. Another week later he had again shot and killed an unarmed police sergeant. Prudom was an ex-British Forces survival expert, and the search for him was the largest armed police manhunt at that time. About 600 police officers including

100 armed officers were combing the forests and rough terrain of the area in the search for him.

We were hardly armed to the teeth to deal with such a violent killer – only with our police batons. We christened ourselves 'The Dispensables' because we reckoned the force wouldn't be too bothered if we were shot. We were all very young in service and most of us were not even qualified police drivers. We spent 2 days trudging through the forest and fields in a line of up to 40 officers with an armed officer after every 10th officer. Our brief was that, if we saw anything suspicious, we would shout 'Down!', and we would all dive to the ground whilst the armed officers dealt with it. Of course, boredom developed after a while and not every 'down' shout was serious. We would shout 'Down!' when one of our colleagues was passing a pond or a cow pat and then laugh our heads off to see them wet through or smelling of cow dung.

Prudom was tracked down and cornered and died in a violent shootout with police, although an inquest later ruled that he died from a bullet shot by his own hand.

CHAPTER 16

JOINING CID

On the 1st of December 1982 I returned to Odsal police station to work in the CID office. I went from being called PC to TDC – Trainee Detective Constable. The position was also referred to as the CID aide. I would be an aide for six months, working with experienced detectives and got the chance to be involved with more serious cases. If I was good enough to make the grade at six months, I would be sent on an initial CID training course for a further four months. This was going to be a gruelling and difficult period and I was well aware that many people before me had failed it. I had no intention of failing to complete the training. I was not going to give anyone any opportunity to make 'thick Irish' jokes at my expense.

The CID framework was much smaller than what I'd been used to. The department was led by a detective chief inspector (DCI) who we didn't see a lot. The day-to-day management was by the detective inspector (DI). There was four small teams of six officers plus a detective sergeant (DS) on each team. Often the officers would be seconded away for long periods on major enquiries and so the teams were reduced. However, the amount of work was the same, and so the officers who remained had to deal with a heavier workload.

The DS on my team was called Bob Adams. The CID is run on a less formal basis than the uniform section. It was acceptable in CID that we would call our DS by his first name. In uniform section it could only be 'Sgt'. The inspector in uniform section would be called 'Sir', but in CID we would get away with calling him 'Boss' or 'Guv'. Even the superintendents in CID were happy to be called 'Boss', and were all very approachable.

Bob was a giant of a man – 6'6" tall and well over 20 stone. His reputation as a top class detective was even bigger and, as luck would have it, he was also a gentleman to work for. I had fallen on my feet to have such a good trainer. The detectives on the team changed from time to time, but I spent most of my time working with a lad called Andy Best who was just a little bit older than me and became my best mate. Andy was a real character and we got up to all sorts of escapades together. I taught him how to speak some Irish and how to sing Irish rebel songs. We stayed friends over the years and he can still belt out a few verses of 'Armoured cars and tanks and guns', and even greet people in Irish.

Although I was part of a small CID team, I came into contact with CID officers from all over West Yorkshire and the UK. Many of them were older and more entrenched in their ways. They were 99% white British and were suspicious of anyone outside the group. I could sense hostility with some of them when they saw my obviously Irish name and heard my Irish accent. Some of them would mimic my accent or tell 'Irish' jokes all in the name of banter and good humour. I realised then that my CID aide-ship was going to be difficult, not just with the serious nature of the work, but with the bad attitudes of some of my new colleagues.

My workload shot up immediately. I was allocated lots and lots of crime to investigate. Because I was the aide, the menial, boring jobs came my way while the older more experienced officers sat in the office drinking coffee, talking of the good old days and waiting for a 'big job' to come in. Some of them would only move when a murder, rape or a shooting came in. Anything below that was left to me and the younger detectives – all in the name of giving us experience.

Deceptions and fraud offences under the theft act could be quite difficult to deal with, and many police officers kept away from them because they didn't understand the law. I became quite adept at these offences because of the number of crimes I had to investigate. The large electrical stores such as Dixons, Comet and Currys had introduced a new way of shopping. It was called instant credit – buy now, take away now, and pay later. The security checks on customers were very basic and every Tom,

Dick and Harry thief was walking out of the stores carrying a new colour TV or video recorder after giving false details. Most of them came my way to investigate when – surprise, surprise – no repayments were made. Most of this equipment was being sold in pubs for a fraction of the price.

About that time I decided I would like to have a new video recorder and, as money was tight, I decided I would buy it on the instant credit scheme. I went to Dixons where I gave my details and waited for a decision to be made. The salesperson came back a few minutes later and said to me – "I'm sorry, you have not qualified, we won't be able to sell it to you on this occasion". My background and credit history were impeccable and I realised straight away that I had been refused credit because of my Irish accent. Irish gypsies had a bad reputation for stealing and it was clear I was being placed in the same category.

Because of my job I knew they were handing out the video recorders to every drug addict and thief in the town and to criminals who could be spotted a mile away. I was working my butt off to recover their property for them and this was the thanks I received. I was angry and asked to see the manager. He couldn't really give me an excuse as to why I had been refused credit, but when I showed him my warrant card, he couldn't get me a video recorder fast enough. And so off I went with my new Beta VCR under my arm.

When I was starting out in CID 30 years ago, people were not as politically correct or as professional as they are now. That era in the police is referred to as the 'life on Mars' period because it was so unreal. Detectives drank coffee, smoked and played cards between big jobs. On a night shift they went into the pubs and clubs, meeting informants and gathering intelligence.

Sgt Bob was not lazy, he carried a large workload as well as looking after his team. He treated everyone well no matter what their ethnicity or background. Sometimes he would call us in when we were working on evenings and ask us what we had to do. I would say I've got to arrest somebody for burglary and I'm looking for someone else for an assault, and Bob would say – "Do that tomorrow, Gerry, I'm taking you to meet some contacts". I knew straight away that meant we were going to some pubs. We then visited a number of public houses in the area. Everyone knew we were CID as we wore smart suits, shirts and ties. In any event, they knew Bob very well.

Bob introduced me to lots of people. Some were landlords and decent customers, some were villains and criminals. It was a great way of getting to know the community. It was also a good way of generating intelligence. People would tell us who was doing what crime in the city. If not there and then, they would make contact with us later. Many an informant was recruited in this way of going into pubs and meeting people. These people respected us for going into their community and it helped break down barriers and make the police more accessible and approachable. It wouldn't be an acceptable way to work today.

Because of my Irish accent, most people referred to me as 'The Irish Detective', and the name stayed with me for 30 years. If someone posted a letter to HQ addressed 'to the Irish Detective', I would get it. The only downside was, if anyone made a complaint about an officer with an Irish accent, then I would be suspect number one. Some people are not too good with differentiating accents. My friend detective Geordie Davison spoke with a strong Geordie accent and some people thought he was Irish, so some of his complaints came my way to the absolute amusement of Geordie.

I learnt from Bob that a good detective needed to be able to adopt a flexible approach to their style of communication. He could be at ease speaking with a bishop or a bank manager one minute, and then lower himself to a tone comfortable to a sex offender, in order to get the best out of that person.

I once had arrested a man for taking a young girl of seven off the street and sexually assaulting her. I had interviewed him several times, but he would not admit it, and it looked like I would have to release him. Bob said he would have a try with me to see if he would admit it. I had been quite formal in my line of questioning, but Bob managed to communicate with the man on his own level. At one stage Bob said to him in a rather sympathetic manner – "look lad, you're not on your own, lots of men have sexual thoughts over young girls". In a few minutes the man had broken down, feeling sorry for himself and fully admitted the offence. A dangerous sex offender was taken off the streets thanks to Bob's expertise in communication.

Because he was such a large man, Bob could be very awkward. The seatbelt law had come in and all our cars had belts fitted. Bob could not get the hang of getting the belt around his large frame and going 'clunk click'. He paid me and Andy overtime to adjust all the cars' seatbelts so that they would go around his large body. Andy and I would also play the 'clunk click' game with Bob. The test was for whichever of us was driving the car to see how far we could travel until Bob finally managed to get his belt on. We could sometimes travel for miles and have reached our destination by the time Bob would finally manage to secure his seatbelt.

The work came in thick and fast and I gained a lot of valuable experience. As the months passed, I also got to deal with the most serious range of incidents. I got a call to a house one dark winter's evening. The male occupant had threatened to harm himself and had not been seen for some days. The house was in complete darkness, but one upstairs window was partly open. I got a ladder from a neighbour and I climbed in the window. None of the lights worked and I had no torch. I decided to make my way downstairs in the dark and take it from there. As I came down the stairs with my hand outstretched to guide me, I felt something by the banister. I had a good feel of the object only to my horror to realise I was feeling somebody's cold head. The man had hanged himself and I had found him in the dark. I can tell you it didn't take long for that brave police officer to get down those stairs.

I learnt a lesson in crime scene management one day when I was called to a house where a woman's body had been found in the kitchen. Crime scenes have to be controlled so that only essential officers go anywhere near them for fear of contaminating the scene. One speck of DNA or a stray hair can foul up a murder investigation. I remained outside the house waiting for further instructions. It was freezing cold and there was snow on the ground. I came closer to the house than I should have and I stood into an outside toilet to keep warm. After a while in the dark I stepped back a bit further and stepped on something that appeared to be a foot. There was a body of a man sitting on the toilet. It didn't half make me jump. As it happened, both deaths were from natural causes and so no evidential problems had arisen.

Another rule of crime scene management is not to touch anything – keep your hands in your pockets with your gloves on. There is an unwritten rule that if a detectives' fingerprints or DNA is found at the scene of a major crime, then that detective will be back in uniform section tomorrow.

On one major enquiry a piece of paper had been left on the boss's desk. I had a good look at it and handled it. Then I heard it was now a crucial piece of evidence in the investigation and it was to be tested for fingerprints. It was so important that it had to be taken down to Scotland Yard where they had the most advanced system in the country for lifting fingerprints from paper. I knew if my fingerprints were found on it, my career in the CID would be over. I waited with bated breath for several days until the result came through from the Yard – no marks of value. On that occasion, I was grateful the system wasn't as good as it had been reputed.

These were valuable learning experiences. I never made the same mistake twice. At the end of my six months attachment to CID I learned I had been classed as successful and I was put forward for the CID course. Another difficult and long course away from home lay ahead of me. A move to CID is not officially a promotion, but just about everyone views it as such. Without any justification whatsoever and very much wrongly, the uniform patrol department is viewed as the bottom rung of the policing ladder, probably, because its officers tend to be the younger end of the staff. It is however very unfair to look down on them, because they are the backbone of the service. They run from pillar to post and have to deal with the less glamorous aspects of the job. In the patrol department you need to have a good knowledge of policing because you can literally be dealing with anything from one moment to another – from a stray horse on the highway to a complex public order situation.

CID was and indeed still is viewed as the attractive and more 'glamorous' side of policing. Not for us rolling about in the gutter on a Saturday night with a violent drunk. We would be more likely to be dealing with a serious crime that would be all over the newspapers and the TV news the following day. We wore a smart shirt and tie and trendy suits with a matching handkerchief in the chest pocket. Some CID officers performing a more undercover role would wear jeans and sweaters and trainers. In those days I had plenty of hair and I was allowed to let it grow as I liked. No more Polish barber head shaves for me.

There can be a lot of jealousy and resentment between different departments within the police. There would be backbiting and petty complaining if one department seemed to be earning more overtime than another, for instance. Some disparaging terms were banded about. Patrol officers were called 'wooden tops', traffic officers were called 'robots' and CID officers were referred to as 'boozers'. Not everyone subscribed to this backbiting. Most did though, and I always thought they were small-minded and let themselves down. I have to say I never looked down on any department. Our overall purpose in life was the same, and we all played an important role in the crusade.

Chapter 17

The CID Course

In July 1983 I went to Bishopgarth training academy at Wakefield to complete the initial CID training course. With only 4 years' service, I was one of the most inexperienced officers on the course. It was a 12 week residential course, but I would get home on each weekend. I was under no illusion that it was going to be anything but easy as I had heard some shocking anecdotes from officers who had been on the course.

There were about 100 students on the course from all over the UK and the Commonwealth. The academy was a purpose-built training centre and had all the facilities we required, unlike the old RAF base where I had completed my initial training. The academy was warm, comfortable and modern. We each had our own en-suite bedroom with radio, TV etc. All of our meals were provided and they even gave us some expenses each Thursday so that we could go up the town and let our hair down. Each day I saw the drill sergeant putting the uniform officers through their paces on the parade ground and shouting at the top of his voice. I thought to myself – "Good riddance to you, Sgt".

My first day at the academy was a Sunday afternoon. We were

instructed to get settled in on the Sunday in order to be ready to start the course first thing on Monday morning. The academy was pretty much like a hotel with a reception, lifts, etc. I went to reception with my suitcase and I said – "Gerry O'Shea, attending the CID course". A large man stood at the desk with the receptionist and he said he was Inspector Bower and he would be in charge of my class. Other inspectors were also present to oversee their students' arrival.

The receptionist handed me a key and in a supercilious manner gave me a lot of information in one long sentence. "Take the lift to floor 7, then room 74. Breakfast at 8am in the dining room on the ground floor, then lecture room 4 by the theatre at 9am". I said – "Can you just repeat that for me" – so that I could digest it. She did so again in an 'I'm bored' tone and I headed for the lift. At the lift I looked back at reception to see Inspector Bower on his knees looking towards heaven and saying – "Why have I got the thick Irish one in my class". I didn't say anything. If I had, it would have made the course even more difficult. I just thought to myself – "Feck you, Inspector, I will prove you wrong".

I never harboured any grudge against that inspector. He was just being juvenile and playing to the crowd. We got on very well during the course and he treated me fairly. He was also good at his job as a CID trainer and imparted a wealth of complex criminal law training unto us.

Like everything else in the police force, the CID course was a most competitive process. The tutors competed with each other to have the best class and of course they piled the pressure on us to produce the goods. We had long, exhausting days of learning followed by exam after exam, and even more revision. Again, I felt added pressure because I knew, if I didn't perform well, I would give them fuel for their 'Irish' jokes and so I worked even harder. At almost every exam I came top of the class.

At the end of the course there was a formal dinner suit event attended by the students' relatives, several bigwigs from the local authority and the senior police management team. There was a final competition to decide the best class on the course and the overall best student of the course. I was selected to represent our class. I won the honour for our class and I also won 'The Student of the Course' award. I received my award from the chairman of the police authority. Inspector Bower was delighted his class had won. It meant a lot to him. Later that evening, after we'd had a few drinks, he congratulated me and thanked me. I said – "Not so much of the thick Irish now then?" He blushed and apologised profusely.

My brain was hurting from the pressures of studying and I had also had to look after my wife and two young boys in the little bit of spare time I had on weekends. I was glad to have the course successfully under my belt and be home again. I had spent the summer months sitting in a classroom and missed out on a summer holiday. So the first thing I did was to take the family across to Ireland for a two week break.

CHAPTER 18

BACK TO ODSAL

In late 1983 after my initial CID course I went back to work at Odsal division. I was brimming full of confidence and awash with a wealth of knowledge about criminal law and procedure. I was confident there was no area of the law that I could not deal with. I was now a qualified detective having worked hard and jumped through all of the hoops placed before me. I knew I could be posted to any CID office throughout the force, but I was keen to stay in the Bradford area to keep my costs and time spent on travelling down.

The CID was an extremely popular department and extremely difficult get a place in – it was basically a case of waiting for dead man's shoes, as most of the staff only moved when they retired, got promoted or dropped in the shit. The selection method for any vacancy was to be in rotation from a succession waiting list. I was third on the list so I expected a lengthy wait.

I went back to uniform patrol, but I was now treated with a great deal of respect owing to my new status as a potential detective and my extensive training. I was appointed the crime manager on the team and dealt with the more serious crimes and helped the other patrol officers with their crime work. In and amongst this I still liked to go out on patrol and attend incidents to help out my colleagues.

Out on patrol one day I came across a queue of traffic at a busy road junction. The junction was controlled by traffic lights and it wasn't usually snarled up like this. I made my way to the front of the queue and was surprised to see what was causing the backup. A woman was standing in the middle of the junction directing the traffic and making a right pig's ear of it. She was waving her arms like a cop on point duty and shouting 'Stop!' and 'Go!' in such an erratic manner that it was a wonder there was not several accidents caused. She was clearly deranged.

I took her arm and gently led her to the pavement, allowing the traffic to get back to normal. I asked her what she was doing and she said she was allowing the cats to cross the road safely. I ran a check on her and the control room told me she was a well-known local eccentric. Her name was Jesse and she lived with her brother, so I decided to take her home to a place of safety. On reaching her small terraced house she opened the door and I was amazed to see the house was full of cats. There must have been about 30 cats in the living room, they were everywhere, and the house smelt stink. Jesse's brother was every bit as mad as what she was. They were under the care of social workers and health workers and were deemed to be okay to live in the community. I left them to get on with it. I would submit a report to social services and ask them to keep an eye on them.

About a week later in the same area of the city a local shopkeeper rang the police to report an unusual theft. I went to see him. The Pakistani gentleman told me he owned a lovely black and white cat that used to sit in the shop and keep him company. A woman had come into the shop and grabbed the cat, stuffed it into her shopping bag and ran away with it. He offered to show me the incident on CCTV, but I said – "Don't bother" – as I had a good idea who was responsible for this case of cat-napping.

I drove straight around to Jesse's house and she let me in. I saw the black and white cat was asleep on a cushion and I asked Jesse where she had got it from. She said – "I bought it in the shop". I decided to take the cat back to the shop, but I had no way of carrying it. I went back to the shop and told the shopkeeper I had got his cat back, but I just needed to borrow something to carry it in. He gave me a cardboard box that had held crisps and away I went to get the cat. The Pakistani shopkeeper was very pleased he was about to get his cat back and the whole family had got together in the shop to welcome the cat back. I was the hero of the hour and was offered Coke and crisps as a reward.

Back at Jesse's house I got the cat and placed it into the box. The cat didn't want to be in the box and went mad trying to get out. As I carried the cat to the police car, it jumped up and forced the top of the box to open. Despite my frantic efforts to hold onto the cat, it jumped out of the box and escaped. The last I saw of that cat was it dodging the wheels of lorries and cars as it ran down the busy highway.

Now I had a big problem. I went back to the shop where the family were eagerly awaiting the return of the stolen cat. I told them how the cat had escaped and tried to make it better by saying it would probably make its own way home. No more Coke and crisps for me this time. I don't know if the cat ever did make it home as I never had the courage to go back – not one of my biggest successes.

They say – never work with animals – and I should have listened to that advice. One day I attended at a woman's house where she reported some type of minor crime to me. The lady was very elegant and the house was nice and clean. She had a small miniature dog with white fluffy fur and a ribbon in its hair. The dog went mad when I entered the house in my uniform. It was barking and yelping and biting at my legs. The lady offered me a cup of tea and assured me not to worry as the dog would not bite me. Unfortunately, she was wrong and the dog sank its sharp teeth into my leg. It really hurt and I reacted instinctively by kicking out at the dog with my size 10 Doc Martens boot. Without meaning to, I kicked him a bit too hard and it caused the little dog to sail across the room like a football, hit the wall and fall down dazed.

The lady was shocked that I had assaulted her 'baby' and the offer of the cup of tea never materialised. I had blood coming out of my leg and my uniform was ripped. I spent half a day at Bradford Royal infirmary, waiting to get injections to counter any infection. Reluctantly, I had to report the lady for keeping a dangerous dog and for damaging my uniform. She had to pay a sum of money to cover repairs and my compensation.

On another occasion I was stopped by a group of people standing outside a house. They told me the lady householder was locked out of her home. She had gone shopping leaving her very large and aggressive Alsatian dog alone inside the house. The dog had jumped up on the front door and had moved the button on the Yale lock causing it to lock, so when the woman came back from the shop, she could not open the door with her key. Luckily, there was an upstairs window open and the neighbours had placed a ladder up to it. They asked me to climb up the ladder, get into the house and open the front door from the inside. I said – "Why don't you do it?", to which they said they were afraid of heights and afraid of the dog.

I could see the dog through the window, it was huge and barking, and snarling with rage. The owner said – "He's just excited, he won't harm you". Never listen to dog owners when they say this to you.

I took off my hat and jacket and climbed up the ladder to the bathroom window. I opened the window fully to climb in. The dog heard me at the window and bounded up the stairs at top speed and stuck his head up to the window, nearly knocking me off the ladder. I told the owner to call the dog to the front door so that I could climb in. The dog responded by running downstairs and attacking the front door.

I quickly climbed into the bathroom and the dog, having heard me, again bounded up the stairs barking loudly. I managed to get to the bathroom door and close it to keep the dog outside. Unfortunately, there was no lock on the door and I had to lean against it with all my weight to keep the ferocious dog out.

Now I was stuck. I couldn't get back to the window because the dog would push in the door and get me and I couldn't open the door because the dog was on the other side. I stayed there for several minutes contemplating my best options. I thought of using my radio to summon help from my colleagues, but I knew I would be a laughing stock and I'd never live it down. I'd rather be eaten by the Alsatian, so I would take my chances with the dog.

There was a small chair in the bathroom and I took hold of it. I gradually opened the door, while at the same time using the chair legs like a lion tamer in the circus to keep the snarling dog at bay. I guided the dog backwards down the stairs while he chewed on the chair legs. At the bottom of the stairs I managed to coax him into the lounge, closed the door and isolated him. Then I opened the front door to the sound of applause from the neighbours. Despite my success on this occasion, I vowed to keep away from animals wherever possible in the future.

I expected to have to wait for at least a year before I was appointed into the CID, so I was surprised when after only four weeks I got a call from a DCI in a neighbouring division asking if I would be interested in filling a vacancy in his department. It was just before Christmas and it was raining and freezing cold. I was directing traffic at a notoriously dangerous junction called Hell Fire Corner where the traffic lights had failed. My arms were tired, I was cold and miserable and I did not have any enthusiasm for what I was doing. I thought about it for two seconds and said – "Yes, I'd love to join you". He invited me for an interview.

CHAPTER 19

THE NEW DETECTIVE

DCI John O'Sullivan was one of the very few other Irish descent officers in the force, and the following week I went to see him at Laisterdyke police station. After a short interview he told me the position was mine. I pointed out there was two other officers in the queue before me and he said in his soft Irish accent – "Don't worry about them", and he gave me a big wink.

The other officers were not happy when they learnt I had jumped ahead of them. But DCI Jonno, as we called him, justified his decision by pointing out I had a higher pass mark and he wanted the best. It was a clear case of positive discrimination in my favour by my fellow Irishman, but I didn't care about that. I was over the moon, I'd had so much negativity because of my nationality that I wasn't about to worry when something went my way.

In January 1984 I was on the road again to a new division to work with new people. Laisterdyke was known as GB CID and covered large areas of Leeds Road, Holmewood, Bierley, East and West Bowling. Like most other areas in the force, it was a busy place to work and was well known for its high rate of serious crime. Most of the detectives were older than me and had considerably more practical experience than me. There were a few other officers near my own age.

In those days the CID was a male-dominated world. There were 2 or 3 female detectives at Laisterdyke. They were very good and could hold their own against any male. One of them called Anne had some Irish blood in her and we got on well and often worked as partners. She was brilliant – sensitive one moment and tough as nails the next, depending on the situation we were dealing with. Most of the staff were very pleasant to me and I knew I would enjoy working there when I settled in. If I didn't fit into the team or I was not accepted by them, my CID career in that division would be short.

The staff were very hard workers in the main and in a difficult policing area, and against all the odds their success rate was tremendous. We worked long hours, often putting ourselves at risk in making arrests for serious crimes and foiling armed raids amongst other things. The team of detectives played hard too. Most of them gambled heavily, smoked heavily and drank even heavier. On reflection, I think the gambling, smoking and drinking was a way of relieving the enormous stresses caused by the job. It was commonplace to go for a drink after work. If you didn't join in the social life of the group as well as the working practices, you would be ostracised. The trick was to be involved with the group in order to promote a good working environment, but not to let the drinking and hard socialising to drag you down. You needed to be made of stern stuff and be well self-disciplined to do this successfully.

With a young family to support I couldn't afford to party hard regularly anyway, even if I'd wanted to. I have never smoked and I wasn't a gambler. I did like a drink, but I was able to control it. I would go for a drink and play darts and pool with the others, but I wouldn't go all the time – and even then I would go home early. I have seen some officers ruin their careers because they were not able to discipline themselves and control their social life. Drink-driving was more acceptable in those days, but yet several officers lost their jobs because of it.

It is much harder to monitor and supervise officers in the CID just because of the type of work they do. They may have to go into pubs, clubs and casinos in the course of their work. They may also have to disappear for hours on end. In this environment you must be strongly self-disciplined and that is something instilled in you from day one. In my time at GB CID, I witnessed a number of officers fall victim to their weak self-control. One young detective got drunk on duty one night and started a fight in a takeaway. He lost his job. Another crashed his car after drinking and again got sacked.

A new Sgt called James came to our department. He was on the succession list to be promoted to inspector and he had been told to get some practical experience of CID work at a divisional level. He was a well-spoken, educated man who was considered to be a 'flyer' – that was a slang word for someone who was going to fly up the ranks. James managed to get on all right with the work side of the CID environment, but he fell foul of the social side. Within a few months he was drinking and gambling to excess. One night when I was the night detective cover and in the office on my own, a rather inebriated James came in. He told me he had been out for a few drinks and had lost his car as it wasn't in the car park. I found his car parked on the next street where he had left it earlier in the day. He intended to drive it home, but I took his keys from him and I gave him a lift home.

Another night we went to a casino to play roulette. I would have a set amount of money that I could afford to lose. And when that was gone, I would stop playing. The gambling bug had got to James though, and he didn't know when to stop. When he had lost most of his cash – and it was a substantial amount – he took his credit card from his wallet and told me to go and withdraw £200 from the mini bank. He even gave me his pin number as he did not want to lose his place at the roulette table. I refused to do it and he got angry and said – "I am ordering you to do it!" I just laughed and put the bank card in my pocket to look after it safely. James was a nice guy, but he couldn't deal with the bad influences around him. He left us soon afterwards and he never did get promoted.

Dealing with informants is another area of a detectives' work that is fraught with danger. The majority of informants are also criminals or are closely associated with them. Let's face it, your average Mr Jones down the road will know nothing about a £1million drugs stash. Nowadays the rules and regulations for dealing with informants are very tight, but in my early years they were not and many officers came to grief with them. There is an old saying – 'if you lie with the dogs, you will catch fleas'. There is a danger that in working closely with informants, who are also criminals, a police officer can turn into a criminal himself. There is a thin line between both activities. Some detectives believe the informant is their friend and can be trusted. That is never the case – informants only provide information for a reason that is beneficial to them in one way or another. Usually it's for financial reward, to get a lighter sentence themselves, or possibly to get revenge on someone else. One officer I knew very well got into such serious trouble over an informant that he actually hanged himself.

I was used to the constant movement of staff within the police force. I was a bit sad still to see my Irish boss Jonno retire. He had been very good to me. My new boss was a completely different kettle of fish altogether. He wasn't nicknamed 'Biff' for nothing.

He could be very aggressive. Equally, he could be an absolute gentleman. We always joked that it depended on where the moon was as he was ruled by it. Whatever his mood though, he was always a first-class manager and top detective. You could rest assured any serious or major crime he commanded would be resolved successfully.

Because of his volatile nature some of the staff hated him while others loved him. He tended to split the camp. I got on very well with him and he taught me an awful lot about police management and higher investigation techniques. He even encouraged me to do my promotion exams because at that stage I was beginning to realise that my ambition to emigrate was unlikely to be achieved.

Despite our good relationship it was inevitable we would have some fallout. He would make a point of having a public fallout in front of other staff, intended I suppose to intimidate them as well. He picked an argument with me one day over some overtime that I had worked. He threatened to cut my overtime, which would equally reduce my wage. I gave as good as I got and one of the sergeants came to me afterwards and said – "Watch your back now, he will have you out".

Lo and behold, a couple of days later an order came from HQ that a detective from our unit was required to work on a major enquiry at Huddersfield. It was a surprise to no one when the DCI came in and told me I was going. I worked at Huddersfield for about two months until the serious investigation was resolved. It was a case of a young woman who was brutally raped by a man posing as a taxi driver. I made an absolute fortune by working long days and most of my rest days as overtime as well. I also got lots of mileage and other expenses allowances. I made a point in going to see the DCI to tell him I was earning a fortune in overtime and did not feel I was being punished. Fortunately, he had his good head on that day and he just laughed and said he wanted me back as soon as possible.

I returned to GB CID to complete my five-year stint there. I was carrying a huge workload. It wasn't unusual to be carrying a daily workload of 30 crimes to investigate. Admittedly, some of them were undetectable and not a lot could be done with them. Many other crimes though were very serious and required an awful lot of work and time. Between dealing with prisoners on an almost daily basis there were court files to type and prepare. Then on top of all that were the regular appearances at the Crown court, the Magistrates court, and the Coroner's court, giving evidence and obtaining search warrants.

I investigated the suspicious death of a man outside a public house in the Holmewood area. A disturbance had taken place inside the pub and a man was ushered outside by the staff and some locals. Outside the door a further scuffle had taken place and the man had ended up at the bottom of a steep flight of concrete steps. He died two days later from a fractured skull. The big question was – was he pushed or did he fall. I spent weeks taking witness statements, forensically examining the scene and obtaining medical reports until I was at a stage where I could arrest three men on suspicion of murder. The suspects were believed to be violent. I also needed to arrest all three at separate locations at the same time in order to preserve forensic evidence. I organised a huge briefing for a 6am swoop.

The Superintendent, the DCI, the DI and the Sergeants were briefed to attend. I had dogs units, uniform staff and fellow detectives organised to attend. I prepared a detailed PowerPoint briefing presentation detailing who was doing what and where. As I had conducted the full investigation on my own, I was the only person with the knowledge to be able to brief the troops.

I can honestly say in over 30 years in the police I was never late for duty until – you guessed it – this important morning. Bad timekeeping is not tolerated in the police. You have to be dependable, but with the worst luck in the whole world I chose that morning to be late. I set my alarm clock for 4am, but for some reason it did not go off. When I eventually opened my eyes to check the time I was horrified to see it was 6:15am. I sprang out of bed like a hare on a promise and got into work at 7am. The car park was full and when I opened the office door there was in the region of 50 police officers of all ranks glaring at me. I sheepishly said "sorry", and made up some whopper of a lie, but it didn't serve to defuse the tension in the room. DCI 'Biff' came forward and in a stern voice said to me – "My office now". We went to his office and he fell about laughing. He said – "If the superintendent asks, tell him I've given you a good bollocking". Despite our late start the operation was a complete success and the superintendent got some brownie points out of it when he gave a press statement to the media.

Many violent incidents I dealt with originated from alcohol or public houses. In the Bierley area a young man had been killed when he was knocked down by a car outside a public house. I was one of the first officers on the scene, but there was nothing I could do to help the man. It looked like a tragic accident – the man had gone into the road and been hit by the passing vehicle.

When I investigated it further, however, I discovered it was not so straightforward. An argument had taken place in the pub over a game of pool. The young man was threatened by someone with a pool cue and, fearing for his safety, he ran across the road to get away whilst being chased by the cue yielding thug. He was hit by the passing motorist who was innocent of all blame. I managed to get a conviction of manslaughter for the offender. The victim's family would have liked a murder conviction, but they understood that the best that could be done had been achieved.

Once I got seconded to a major crime incident in another division. An old lady who lived alone in a large detached house had been savagely attacked with an axe and murdered. The first thing I did, as with all other serious crimes, was to visit the scene to get a feeling for the job. The house was a bloodbath and it was obvious the old lady had no chance of surviving the attack. One of the items stolen from the victim's house was a large portable radio cassette player. It was recovered, having been dumped by the murderer not far from the scene. An unusual thing about it was the electrical cord had been cut and part of it was missing.

As the days went by, our murder squad identified a good suspect until we were pretty sure he was responsible. He was a local youth. The youth was arrested and interviewed by my colleague detectives. He denied anything to do with the killing over several days of interviews. My partner and I were detailed to go search the suspect's house for any possible evidence. In his bedroom we seized some clothing and footwear that could possibly link him to the scene. When we were searching his bedroom, I got that cold sensation come over me again, and I felt there was something in the room that disturbed me. Nevertheless, we didn't find anything else and we returned to the incident room where we dealt with the items we had seized as exhibits. We then talked about the search, but I did not mention my 'cold sensation' feeling. For some reason we decided to go back to the house again and have another look.

We focused on the bedroom where I had sensed the strange feeling. Hidden in and amongst some bed clothes in the wardrobe we found an electrical lead that had been cut. We took the cable back to the incident room and it was forensically examined. It made a perfect match to the stolen radio cassette player from the victim's house. This piece of crucial evidence helped to persuade the suspect into making a confession that he was responsible for killing the old lady.

CHAPTER 20

BRADFORD CITY DISASTER

One terrible tragedy I will never forget took place on Saturday 11 May, 1985. I was due to start work at 5pm until 1am the following morning in the CID. I spent the afternoon before work lazing about the house and watching the Saturday sport on television. Bradford City football club had won the football league third division trophy that season. Their game against Lincoln City that day took place in a celebration atmosphere with the team being presented with the trophy. It was a full house in the stadium. I would normally have been at the game, but I hadn't gone because I was working that evening.

I was watching the sports highlights on television between having a cup of coffee and getting ready for work. Then the TV pictures showed a fire breaking out at the stadium. Initially I thought it would be nothing, but then it developed into an inferno and people with burning clothes could be seen running onto the pitch. I got to work at 5pm and very soon afterwards I was directed to get to the Valley Parade stadium to assist with the fire emergency.

It was many hours later when the fire was extinguished that the full scale of the horror was unveiled. 56 men women and children had died in the fire and hundreds more had been seriously injured. I would not wish to recreate what I saw at the scene of that horrific fire as it would not achieve anything here, and would be quite upsetting for many people. I will, however, always remember the scenes that I witnessed that night. There are not many other jobs in the world where you have to deal with such harrowing tragedies – not everybody can cope with dealing with such an event. The tragedy brought a huge dark depression over the whole city of Bradford and it led to major new safety standards in all UK football grounds. The stadium was rebuilt as a modern, fit for purpose soccer arena, and re-opened in December 1986.

In the period when Valley Parade stadium was closed, Bradford City played most of their games at Odsal Stadium. This brought more work my way as it was in my division. I was involved in an investigation where a mini riot had taken place inside the stadium. In the worst possible taste, during the commotion, someone set fire to a catering van at the back of a stand. In view of the recent fire tragedy people were repulsed by this and the incident received widespread media coverage. Using CCTV I managed to identify and arrest the offender.

Football violence was the norm in those days and we always expected trouble on match days. Most of it was minor and was dealt with by the uniform section. Odsal Stadium was primarily a rugby venue and violence was very rare there.

Another Saturday afternoon soccer match saw me involved in a murder enquiry at the stadium. A fracas had taken place among groups of rival supporters leaving the stadium. When they dispersed, a young man was found on the ground, suffering from stab wounds. I was one of the first officers to arrive at the scene. The man died soon afterwards in hospital. The scene was total confusion with thousands of fans milling about. Once again arrests were made and convictions secured at court.

Yet another football-related violent incident took place on another Saturday afternoon when I was on duty. Bradford City was still playing at Odsal Stadium and large groups of supporters were making their way to the stadium, walking up Manchester Road from the city centre and the train station. A small number of uniformed police officers were escorting them, trying to prevent them from fighting with each other. One PC, somewhat ill-advisedly, went into the middle of one large group of rowdy men to calm them down. The group turned on him and punched and kicked him to the ground. A uniformed police inspector was the only officer nearby and he went to the assistance of his colleague. The inspector was not young and was getting to the back end of his service. He was no match for the dozen or so youths who attacked him. He was viciously assaulted before the group ran away.

When I got there, I saw he was so badly injured, I feared it might prove fatal, so I got an ambulance very quickly and I travelled with him on 'blues and twos' to the Bradford Royal Infirmary. The inspector was in a bad way, but eventually made a full recovery. He was off work for several months recovering. Luckily, the PC whom he tried to help was only slightly hurt.

I got to know the inspector very well over the next few weeks while I was getting detailed information from him and keeping him updated. He was one of the nicest persons I have ever met, and I wondered what the football hooligans had hoped to achieve by almost killing him. The inspector never gave much hope for my chances of tracking down the offenders – there had been so many people involved and any witnesses were reluctant to help the police for fear of reprisals. It did prove difficult, but, against all the odds, I managed to identify, arrest and convict most of the yobs who had assaulted him. They were all sent to prison.

Chapter 21

Promotion

By late 1988 we bought our own house and had moved out of the police house. My dream of emigrating was now only a memory. I didn't mind, I was doing what I wanted to do and I was enjoying it very much.

I had taken my DCI's advice and I had been studying hard for my promotion exams. I successfully passed part one of the exams and soon followed that up by clinching part two as well. This involved a lot of hard work and dedication as each exam needed the best part of a year's studying. I then went and sat my part three interview and exam which was the final hurdle leading to promotion. Again, I successfully completed and passed that test.

It was difficult studying for long periods, attending courses, working long hours and looking after a home and young family as well.

During these exams my score had placed me amongst the top 200 candidates in the UK. This was considered to be a real achievement and was used to identify potentially high flying senior officers. I was offered the opportunity to go on an accelerated promotion scheme. This meant I would have to spend a lot of time away from home on courses, learn to speak posh and in return get a good opportunity to progress up the ranks faster. I made some enquiries and was told they liked candidates to be readers of The Times. As I was a reader of The Sun, I declined the offer and decided to take my chances as I was. I never regretted that decision. I don't believe in pretending to be something you are not.

And so it was that after more than five years as a detective constable I was promoted to the rank of sergeant in March 1989. I fully expected, as was usual in those circumstances, that I would be promoted to uniformed sergeant and would return to uniform patrol supervision duties. I had no control over where I would be posted, but I hoped it would be in the Bradford area, for ease of travelling. It was also the area I was more familiar with and comfortable working in.

With a few other officers I lined up in the Chief Constable's plush office in Wakefield. The Chief came down the line shaking our hands and congratulating us. He followed that up by announcing our transfer destination. After shaking my hand he said – "Congratulations, you're going to Weetwood division". I was gob smacked. Weetwood was miles away on the other side of Leeds. I didn't know the area and I didn't know a soul who worked there.

Although I was disappointed, I tried to smile, thanked him, and got on with it.

Next it was back to the stores department to be issued with another shed full of uniform and equipment. A further three weeks residential course at the HQ training academy followed. I can't recall seeing my – not so favourite – drill pig. I think he may have retired. Anyway, I wasn't sorry. After 10 years in the force the anti-Irish sentiments I had endured for years had very much disappeared. The penny had dropped that it wasn't right to hold such racist attitudes against any section of society.

I was not encountering any discrimination at work. When someone did mention an 'Irish' joke, it seemed to be said as a genuine attempt at a joke rather than a vitriolic putdown. Even the television and newspapers were now more informed, and racial discrimination was becoming rare. From the day of my promotion this race related issue rarely raised its ugly head again. Also, I was now in a position of authority and, I have no doubt, this helped. The police service is a disciplined force and authority is respected. Well worth all the effort of studying, I often thought to myself.

In my new uniform with shiny sergeants' stripes on the sleeves, I made my way across Leeds to my new posting at Weetwood division. It was a modern purpose-built police station set in its own grounds on the edge of the city. There was that awkward feeling of not knowing anyone, and the small problem of finding my way around the division. My new A–Z map of the area would be well used in the coming weeks.

My new team at Weetwood was an exceptional group of people. With the exception of one probationer, they were all well experienced. Even the probationer was a graduate and was performing very well. Most importantly for me, they made my settling-in period go without a hitch.

My first week was on night shift; for some reason that often seemed to be the case when I transferred anywhere. My spotlessly clean uniform lost its shine on my second night when a report of a house fire with a person trapped came in. I was doubled-up with a patrol driver who knew the area and we were first on the scene, even before the Fire Brigade arrived. Smoke and flames were bellowing from the house. I kicked the front door open and in the dark choking smoke made a search of the downstairs area with no gain. The fire was centred upstairs, but it was impossible to go up without breathing equipment because of the thick choking smoke. The Fire Brigade arrived in a few minutes and they took control. They found the body of an elderly man upstairs. The fire had been caused by him smoking a cigarette in bed.

My extensive in-depth knowledge of crime investigations was

a tremendous help to me and I was able to improve the team's performance in this area. Soon we were easily the most effective team in the division. The only problem I encountered with working at Leeds was the amount of time spent travelling and the cost of petrol. The ring road was always busy and it took me ages to get there and back. In an effort to save money on petrol I bought myself a motorcycle which reduced costs and also made it easier to get through the traffic. The only problem with the motorcycle was the bad weather. Before I would leave home each morning I would check the road wasn't too icy for the bike, but invariably conditions would change en route and I often came across treacherous conditions on the road. So much so that I fell off the motorcycle 2 or 3 times and that persuaded me to hang up my motorcycle helmet and opt for the safety of a car before I killed myself.

My stint at Weetwood division was to be a relatively short one. I had strong ambitions to get back into CID at the first opportunity. It was extremely difficult to get into CID as a supervisor – again, it was the long waiting time for a vacancy to occur. You also needed to be an experienced detective and there would be a competitive, gruelling interview process to undergo. In addition to all this, your face needed 'to fit' and it helped if you were known to the CID hierarchy and had a good reputation. My problem was that, as I was working in Leeds, no one actually knew me as a detective whereas in the Bradford and western area of the force I was well-known and had a good reputation. I placed a transfer request to return to Bradford on uniform duties in order to increase my chances of a CID place. After 4 months at Leeds I managed to secure a place as a patrol sergeant back at Odsal in Bradford.

One of the traditions in the police is you must have a 'do' when you move or get promoted. You put on a buffet, buy some drinks and everyone comes to wish you well. Someone – usually one of the bosses – gives a speech with a funny slant to it and they present you with a memento. You can usually guess how popular you are by the value of the present as it is all done by someone collecting donations from your colleagues.

I have a cabinet full of treasured engraved glasses, vases and watches that all mean a great deal to me. The beautiful vase I was presented with when leaving Leeds was engraved – 'From Weetwood Team 4 – where did we go wrong' – referring to my short tenure with them.

Chapter 22

Back To Bradford

In July 1989 I made my way back to Odsal police station as a uniform patrol sergeant. It was very much like coming home again – I knew most of the people in the station and I knew the area like the back of my hand. Most importantly, I was back in the eye of the CID's managers and I felt I was better placed to get back into CID as a detective sergeant when the opportunity came along.

My plan seemed to be working when, after a few months, I was asked to lead a newly formed team to combat specific crime problems. The team covered the whole district and I was now reporting to every divisional commander in the Bradford area, I was really in the spotlight where I wanted to be. In the main, we combated auto related crime, drugs and burglary. We worked in plainclothes and drove unmarked cars and worked very closely with the CID. We were very effective in what we were doing, and it got us noticed. As the leader of the team, it did me a power of good and raised my personal profile considerably.

As the months passed by, no vacancies came to light in my area. I was beginning to get a little frustrated, so I widened my search area to the whole of the western part of the force. A position for a DS came up in the Child Protection Unit at Halifax. I decided to apply for it and I got an interview which I passed with flying colours.

Because of the type of work involved, such as dealing with sexual and physical abuse of children, I also had to undergo a psycho analysis test to confirm my suitability for such a delicate role. Not everyone is suited to dealing with harrowing crime committed against children. If you are not of a strong personality, it can have a detrimental effect on you. So I had to answer intrusive questions such as (a) did I like my mother and (b) did I ever have any sexual feelings towards children. Not surprisingly, I managed to pass that test as well, and was offered the job. I gave one month's notice in at Bradford and told them I had secured a detective sergeant's job elsewhere.

Soon afterwards, I got a call from one of the chief inspectors in charge of a CID unit in Bradford. He told me one of his DSs was due to retire in about two month time. If I stayed in Bradford, he assured me that the position would be mine. I wanted to stay in a divisional CID unit, it was exactly what suited me, so I agreed to wait and I turned down the position in the Child Protection Unit . I continued to work hard with my team for the next couple of months. The DCI was happy, he had retained me and I was doing wonders for his crime stats and making him look good.

Then I heard the DS was retiring and I waited for my call. I waited and waited, but nothing happened. Then I heard that another officer had been drafted in from an outside division and he was taking the vacancy. I was fuming, I had missed one opportunity to wait for this, and now it had been given to someone else who was further down the waiting list than me. I went to see the DCI and asked him what was going on. He looked embarrassed and apologised. He told me the Freemasons had pulled the rug from under him. A senior officer who was a Freemason had insisted the outsider, who was also a Mason, was to get the job. There was nothing he or I could do about it. I felt angry, I'd had years of discrimination because I was Irish, and now the Freemasons had dumped on me as well.

The Masonic movement was very popular in the police service in those days. Appointments, promotions and transfers were often influenced by it. I was well aware of the Masons and all the good work they did for the underprivileged. Many of my friends were, and still are members. In time I forgave them for cheating me out of my promised position.

I learnt the lesson that there is often no loyalty in the police. Many senior officers will use you to feather their own nest and then discard you when they do not need you. I vowed that the next opportunity I got, I would take it and I would be off, I would put myself first.

The opportunity came quite quickly when a vacancy came up in the Eccleshill division in Bradford North. I applied for the post and was invited for an interview to Eccleshill police station. This was a large fairly new building in a part of the city that was not well known to me. As always, I revised for the interview and brushed up on the topics I guessed I could be examined on. I also enquired about who was going to interview me, to find out their particular style of interviewing. The chief inspector of the CID and the business manager was to conduct the interview. Neither of them was known to me. I was told the DCI was a 'grumpy old bugger' who was extremely hard to please. The business manager was a well-respected lady who was known to be good at her job.

My preparation paid off, I had a good interview and I was offered the position of a detective sergeant at Bradford north. The DCI who interviewed me was called PJ, and he remained my boss for a few years until he retired. It was true he could be grumpy, and he didn't suffer fools gladly. His staff management skills sometimes left things to be desired, but he was always a good detective and manager, and very loyal to his CID roots. I got on very well with him usually, but now and again, we would have our disagreements. If he ever tried to criticise me, I would say – "It's your fault, because you appointed me" – and he would laugh.

The business manager was a lady called Sue. She had lots and lots of experience and kept the division on course with financial budgets, staff numbers etc. Business managers are a vital cog in the running of every police division. They are always civilians. Unfortunately, many of them were pretty much useless at their jobs, but some – like Sue – were very good.

In my earlier days, the business managers came through the civilian ranks and took many years to reach the elevated position of manager. By that time, they were on a par with the rank of a senior police officer and would be skilled in areas of accountancy and human resources. By the time I had finished in the service, most of these experienced and mature managers had gone. They were now replaced by people with little knowledge or qualifications in the competencies required for the role. It was almost criminal to see how they squandered and wasted money, and how they had no idea of how to deal properly with staff personnel issues.

It was commonplace to go 11 months of the year with our belts tightened, hardly able to spend a penny, only to have to spend thousands and thousands of pounds in the last month of the financial year because of bad finance management. The money would be squandered and wasted on any frivolous project just so that it would not be 'lost' at the end of the financial year. There is surely a case to be made for appointing well-qualified and experienced business managers for such an important role.

CHAPTER 23

ECCLESHILL DIVISION

In February 1991 I made my way to Eccleshill police station at Bradford North. This CID department was large and modern. The Department was made up of male and female detectives of a wide range of experience. Again, I had the difficulty of being new to the area and knowing very few people there. The staff, however, were very welcoming and made me settle in easily enough.

I came into contact with all of the staff at the division, uniform, civilians and CID detectives. I had my own team of detectives and I worked shifts alongside them. They were all mature, intelligent police officers and although they would swap and change periodically, I was to work closely with them for some years to come. I still remain good friends with most of them to this day – John Harrison, John Robinson, Gary Baines, Nigel Spencer and many others. I also met a most charismatic detective called Neil Davison who went by the name of 'Geordie' because of his north east roots and strong Geordie accent. I worked and socialised with Geordie for many years and he also is still a good friend. Geordie was a great detective and a tremendous personality as well. His cheeky and a little mischievous outlook on life made our department a happier place to work.

I had now been in the police for almost 12 years and already I had seen some major changes take place. The 1984 Police and Criminal Evidence Act (PACE) had introduced new police regulations. It change the whole way we conducted investigations, conducted prisoner interviews and dealt with identification issues. Now all contact with prisoners at the police station was either recorded on CCTV or by audio tape. We were governed by strict timelines in which to either charge the suspects or release them.

The process of identifying a suspect by photographs, identification parades and biologically (DNA and fingerprints) had also changed dramatically. There is no doubt whatsoever that these were changes for the better. They were intended to safeguard the rights of the public and to prevent miscarriages of justice, and that can only be a good thing. It was pretty much 'back to school' for us police officers as we had to learn a whole new way of policing, and to learn fast. It had the effect of creating a wider minefield for police officers to overcome to get a case to court. All a defence lawyer had to do was to find a loophole in the complex new legislation – and there were plenty of them – and the defendant would walk free, whether guilty or not. Along with many of my colleagues I was very adaptable and soon got to grips with the new act.

An even more important sea change continued with regard to behaviour and attitudes within the service. Indeed, not only the police service, but the UK as a whole had eventually woken up to the fact that it was absolutely wrong to be seen to discriminate against any section of the community because of their nationality, race, colour, or religion. Our TV screens and the print media were now more selective in their content. The negatively stereotyped 'Irish' joke was becoming a thing of the past. It was like a breath of fresh air too within the police. My new colleagues at Bradford North were great to work with. I have quite a good sense of humour, and we used to have a good laugh and a joke in between the serious side of our business. But our humour was well-meaning and never aimed or intended to upset anyone. Some people might say the reason I was not hearing anti-Irish sentiments now was because I was in a position of authority and people would fear sanctions if they did it to my face. I admit there might be a little truth in this, but I always kept my ear to the ground and I knew all that was happening in any event. If it was going on behind my back, I would have known.

The CID had cleaned up its act too. The hard drinking, hard gambling, macho culture was gone. The 'Life on Mars' era had ended. This was clearly reflected in my new place of work. There was now an increase in the number of female staff in the unit. This had the positive effect of making the men watch their language and their behaviour. My new colleagues did not drink or gamble to excess. There was no more drinking on night duty or going to the pub after work. Instead we went to the gym, trained under weights and played football and badminton. During our lunch breaks we went running for miles. The whole culture had changed and the vast majority of the staff had changed with it. Anyone who breached our tight disciplinary code was dealt with very severely. The cultural changes made my job as a supervisor much easier, the staff were professional and mature enough to look after themselves. I didn't have to go searching for them in pubs, clubs or casinos.

My overall plan was not to spend too long in the rank of sergeant. I thought I would try to get promoted again after two or three years. I had such an interesting time as a DS though, that I was to remain in the rank for nearly 12 years. I had a great team of officers around me, I was on a reasonably good salary, and I could pick and choose the jobs I dealt with. I attended training courses with great regularity. West Yorkshire police made sure we were trained and equipped to perform our role to the highest level. I kept going back to the Academy for advanced training in legislation and police procedures. I was trained in media awareness and media interviews as I would use the local TV and newspapers on a daily basis to seek information on serious crime and to give crime prevention advice to the public. I completed computer and IT courses, self-defence, first aid, risk assessments, and fire marshalling courses. I was so highly trained, I felt like Superman.

From day one at training school we were actively encouraged to compete. In the real world of policing it was no different. I wanted to work in the division with the best reputation in the force. Within the division I wanted to be the top department and within the department I wanted to have the best team and be the best detective myself. I pushed and encouraged my team and they responded by producing excellent results.

By now I had two more additions to my family. Two more sons – Sean, born in 1989, and Aidan, born in 1991. I was well on my way to having my own five aside football team. My four lads were my pride and joy. Money was tight and between work and home responsibilities I was kept busy. To supplement my income, I worked some of my rest days doing 12 hour shifts on overtime. Some of the prisons were affected by industrial actions and prisoners were being kept at police stations instead.

Our cell complex was full of prisoners from Strangeways prison at Manchester. It made for some light relief away from my usual stressful role to look after the prisoners on my rest days and the extra cash was really useful. In addition to our regular holiday trips to Ireland we also went abroad for a sunshine holiday at least a couple of times a year. I wasn't working hard to save money – I wanted the kids to have a good time and to enjoy their childhood.

I had got the bug for enjoying holidays abroad in the sunshine just by luck. Lots of my friends had been raving about their sunshine holidays and all I had experienced was rainy days in Ireland, Scotland or England. Then I was lucky enough to win £1500 in a lottery at work. The household bills were mounting up at home, but I said – "Forget about them for 2 weeks, we're all off to Spain". That first holiday abroad was fantastic and ever since then our family are regular trippers all over the world. Although our default destination and our most popular place is still Ireland.

Crime is a thriving industry and it was rare to have a quiet day. My day started with me getting to work before the rest of the team, I would have looked at the overnight crime and would brief the staff on crimes and incidents of note when they arrived. Then I would allocate the work out for investigation to individual officers and their partners. There would be the run of the mill jobs of assaults, robberies, burglaries and deceptions. If there were any prisoners left in the cells, they would also need to be dealt with.

Our scheduled day shift was usually 9am to 5pm, but the reality was that I just never knew when I would get home. When I was dealing with prisoners, I was up against the PACE clock and I could not go home and leave them, I had to stay to the end. Consequently, I would always try to avoid making plans or arranging to go to events because quite often I couldn't keep them. This can be very frustrating if you have booked to go out or to go to a party, but this is the way of life in the police and you just get used to it.

Chapter 24

Serious Crime

In and amongst the more routine jobs I was also at the forefront of the more serious investigations. Some major crimes I dealt with did not prove difficult to identify who the perpetrator was. Some of them just gave themselves up straight away and confessed, yet it is still a long and complex procedure to bring such a case to the Crown Court and get a conviction. While people may initially admit to killing someone, by the time they get to court, they will plead not guilty for one legal reason or another, or on the advice of a barrister. When the dust has settled and you are looking at the prospect of spending 15 years in a small cell, it can have the effect of making you reconsider your options.

I attended at a house in Eccleshill one afternoon to a report of an elderly lady having been seriously wounded. At the house I was met by a man, who was holding a large kitchen knife. He handed me the knife voluntarily and said – "She is there", pointing to an old lady on the ground. The frail woman in her 80s was suffering from a ferocious stab wound to the stomach and it was a wonder she was still alive. I gave her first aid as best I could to keep her alive until the paramedics arrived, but at the same time I kept one eye closely on the knifeman in case he should become violent again. Other officers attended and took away the knifeman. It transpired he was actually the old lady's son and he was suffering from a serious mental illness. He told me he had heard voices in his head instructing him to kill his mother, although there was never any disharmony between them. He had gone into a shop and bought a large kitchen knife and then attacked her. He was subsequently detained in a psychiatric hospital. His mother made a recovery, but it still had a devastating effect on her and, I'm sure, shortened her life. It was not just the injury, but the fact her own son had hurt her.

Most tragedies affect whole families and not just the victim and the offender. I have dealt with many killers in my time, some were dangerous murderers with the most evil intent. This Asian man was the most polite, and in all other respects, the quietest killer I ever came across. I attended a call early one morning from a man who told the emergency operator – "I have killed my son-in-law". I arrived and found a middle-aged Asian man waiting for me outside the house. He handed me a kitchen knife with blood on it and said – "My son-in-law is dead. I have killed him". I found the body of a young man in the living room with stab wounds. There was nothing I could do to help him, he was already dead.

It was in effect an 'honour' killing, where the head of the Asian family used the ultimate violence to save the honour of his family. He had agreed to an arranged marriage between his daughter, who lived and worked in Bradford, to this young man who lived in India before he came to the UK. The wedding took place and the young man came to live in Bradford with his new wife. It is their culture that the man provides for his wife and family, but the new son-in-law did not do so. The girl's father told him several times that he must get a job, but he did not. Eventually, the father had argued with him and stabbed him to death. Whilst he regretted the killing to an extent, he still felt justified in doing it.

Often there are no winners, only losers in the criminal justice system and the police get caught in the middle. I dealt with a case of an assault and threats on a young woman by her boyfriend. There was some history of alleged offending by the young man against the woman and the latest assault was an offence committed whilst he was on bail for previous incidents. In these circumstances, the general rule to protect the safety of the victim is that the defendant is remanded in custody to prison to await trial at a later date. This is what happened in this particular case. Sadly, while on remand, the young man hanged himself in his prison cell. His family was distraught as was the girlfriend. No one ever wanted this to happen.

I was a regular visitor to one dysfunctional family in the area. A gentleman was doing his best to bring up his family, but the teenage sons and daughter kept letting him down. They took drugs and stole from everyone and anyone including their father. When I first had cause to search their house for drugs and stolen property, I was saddened to see every cupboard, wardrobe and drawer in the house had locked padlocks fitted to them. The father had to lock everything away from his offspring, or they would simply steal it. What a terrible way to live.

The cold sensation of warnings I had experienced had been on an irregular basis, sometimes not happening for many months. In my new role I was dealing with death and dangerous incidents on an almost daily basis and the feelings were becoming more and more common. So much so that I regarded them as my 'sixth sense' asset. I respected these warnings and never dismissed them.

I came on duty one day and I learnt of the death of a young girl of 17 years. She had been found dead in a sleeping bag in a flat on a local housing estate. One of the other CID teams had conducted the initial investigation. The young girl had a history of drug abuse and she had just moved into her own flat. I was told there were no suspicious circumstances and it was probably a drug induced death. I visited the flat with one of my detectives. The girl did not have time to furnish it so there was very little to see. While in the flat I got the strongest feeling of evil that I'd experienced so far. I knew there was something wrong and we spent hours and hours reviewing the circumstances of the death.

When the body was found, the door to the flat had to be forced open. It had been securely locked by mortice lock, but no key was found within the flat. This meant that someone had been in the flat with the girl and had left, locking the door behind them and taking the key with them. This line of enquiry led me to the girl's boyfriend. I questioned him and I had the feeling that he was not telling the truth. I wasn't happy with his denials and I arrested him on suspicion of her murder. Interview after interview, he continued to deny any involvement but my sixth sense was telling me – 'Don't believe him'. I would normally have admitted defeat and released him, but I persevered and I interviewed him further. Eventually, the young man admitted to being in the flat and strangling the girl, he claimed he did not mean to kill her, and he was later convicted of her manslaughter. I was glad I had followed my instinct and had been guided by a good source.

A 75-year-old lady called Margery lived alone in the Undercliffe area of Bradford. She lived in a large old house, but slept downstairs in the living room because she was unable to climb the stairs. In the middle of the night she was awoken by an intruder. In the semi-darkness she saw the figure of a person dressed all in black and carrying a long bladed knife and wearing a hood with holes cut out for the eyes. The intruder knelt across the old lady in the bed and stabbed her several times in the chest and throat. The attacker then fled the scene and left the old lady for dead.

I attended the house the following morning, and there was blood everywhere, which indicated that it had been a very violent encounter. The victim told the ambulance crew that she knew who had attacked her as she was able to recognise them from the voice, but had not been able to talk any further. She was now in the intensive care unit at the Bradford Royal Infirmary and the prognosis was that she was likely to die from her injuries.

I went with another detective to see her in hospital. By a coincidence, the other detective was a fellow countryman of Irish descent. We were allowed to see Margery, and I too thought she was dying. I was desperate to get some kind of declaration from her as to who it was she thought had attacked her. We waited for hours and then she regained consciousness. I sat on the edge of the bed and gently coaxed her to talk to me. She looked up, and several times she said – "It's… it's… it's…", and then faded away. I said – "It's all right, Margery, tell me". Then she said – "It's… it's… it's my leg, you're sitting on it". Then I realised that maybe she wasn't going to die after all… With a bit more coaxing Margery told us that the person responsible was her next-door neighbour – a woman in her 30s. This lady had a key to the house and used to come to see her during the day and generally look after her.

I arrested the neighbour and recovered the blood-stained knife. I also recovered the hood and dark clothing, which turned out to be black bin liners cut to shape. The woman admitted the attack and received a lengthy prison sentence. She never did explain why she had done it. My investigations suggested that she thought she was mentioned in the victim's will and she wanted to hurry things up. The old lady eventually made a good recovery from her terrible injuries. We became good friends and I visited her regularly for several years until her death, and never sat on her leg again.

The best time to arrest someone is when they are off their guard and not expecting it. Early morning raids were a common feature of our routine. The suspects were more likely to be at their place of sleep, catching them fast and unaware meant they were least likely to be prepared to fight or gain access to weapons. It also gave us an advantage when searching for and recovering evidence such as drugs or firearms.

I took my team to Bradford Moor early one morning to arrest a man who was well-known to us as being capable of extreme violence. He was wanted for a violent assault on another man who's ear he had bitten off. We had a good idea he would not come with us easily and he could have access to weapons. I placed officers to the rear and front of the house in case he did a runner. I knocked on the front door loudly – no reply – so I knocked even louder. The upstairs bedroom window opened and the suspect showed himself. I shouted – "Open the front door now or I will put the door in!" Hearing my accent, the man shouted back – "Fuck off you Irish bastard!" I wasn't too pleased with this response, to say the least, so I shouted again – "I'll give you two minutes, if not, the door goes in!" Again, he replied – "Fuck off Irish twat".

I am almost sure I counted down the full 120 seconds, but maybe not any more than that. I then gave the "force entry" order, and one of my men smashed the lovely new UPVC double glazed door down with a battering ram. We dashed inside, overcame the man after some struggle, and took him away. To the embarrassment of the thug in front of his neighbours, he was brought from the house in his underpants, trussed up like a sheep about to be sheared. Along with a criminal charge of assault, he now also had the problem of explaining to his landlord how the front door got smashed. He would have to foot the bill to have it repaired. Maybe the next time he would learn to open the door and desist from using racist language to a sensitive Irishman.

CHAPTER 25

THE MISSING BODY

Some of my team and I were in the CID office late one night preparing reports and doing some clerical work. In the old days we would have been in the pub, but this was the new professional CID. As always, our police radios were switched on and we were monitoring what was happening in the division. In and amongst all the routine calls one call got our attention. It was to a uniform patrol unit – "Please go see a woman who is reporting her daughter missing". Now, missing from home reports are usually ten a penny. People don't come home when expected for a variety of reasons, and usually turn up the next day. But the next part of the message made us concentrate further. It went – "She has been having trouble with her boyfriend recently and her mother is worried".

One of my detectives got on the computer database and did some research. The missing woman lived in Shipley. She had last been seen in Bradford city centre during the evening, drinking. She had been in a stormy relationship with a local man who during the course of an argument with her recently had discharged a shotgun close to her. Normally, 'missing from home' reports would be left with the uniform section to make the initial enquiries for at least 24 hours, but my intuition told me this was a case for CID immediately. We made enquiries at every address she could be at, but there was no trace of her.

We ascertained she was last seen leaving a public house in the city centre with her ex-boyfriend. When we spoke to him, he said he had left her in town. Despite large scale searches and appeals to the media, the woman could not be located. The enquiry was upgraded to a murder investigation led by the highly competent Detective Superintendent Tony Whittle. The boyfriend was the obvious suspect, but we had very little evidence and no body.

It was a long, complex investigation which dragged on for weeks. Eventually we got the breakthrough we had been working so hard for. As a direct result of appeals on the TV news, the boyfriends' car was recovered from a scrapyard. Inside the vehicle we discovered traces of blood and body tissue. A pathologist was able to link the missing woman to the blood and tissue by her DNA even though we had no body. He was also able to conclude that the woman was indeed dead, due to the nature of the body tissue and blood in the car. We also had an amazing sighting of the suspect driving his car soon after the murder in a remote area of the Yorkshire Dales in North Yorkshire. A road worker who was cleaning the roadway saw so little traffic in his quiet area that he actually remembered seeing the suspect in his car and even made a note of the registration number.

The boyfriend was arrested, but denied all knowledge of the crime. Our detailed investigation had revealed his story of events to be a concoction of lies. We suspected he may have disposed of the victims' body in the remote moors, and we searched them extensively. I spent several days hovering over the wild moors in X99 – the police helicopter – but without success.

The case went to trial at the Crown Court. The problem we had was we had a charge of murder, but had no body. The defence suggested the woman was not dead at all but had gone abroad to live in a foreign country, but we had amassed overwhelming evidence against the man; he was convicted of murder and sentenced to life imprisonment. The case made us national headlines in the UK for securing a murder conviction in the absence of a body.

The victim's family had been very close and were devastated by her murder. Although we managed to bring some sense of justice to their lives in securing a conviction of murder, the body was still missing and they wanted it to be found and put her to rest, and I felt bad that we weren't able to achieve that. Even after conviction the defendant would not reveal what he had done with the body. He will never disclose it now because he died in prison while serving his life sentence.

Chapter 26

The Canal Murder

On a bright sunny day in August 1977 a 39 year old woman called Mary walked to work at a local textile mill at Shipley near Bradford. She had left her family at home to take the picturesque walk along the towpath of the Leeds-to-Liverpool canal. The River Aire runs through the valley alongside the canal at that point. Mary never arrived at work and when she did not return home that night her husband reported her missing. The next day her body was recovered from the river. She had been battered, sexually assaulted and strangled. The initial murder enquiry team took over 1300 statements and interviewed about 9500 people. Unfortunately, the killer was not identified. This was in 1977, before I joined the police, but I remembered reading about the case. It was to become West Yorkshire's longest running murder hunt and I would play a major role in resolving it.

A detective sergeant on the original murder team was now my Detective Superintendent called Brian Taylor. Brian had progressed over the years to become one of the best senior detectives in the force. He had everything going for him – well presented, good-looking, charming, excellent at interacting with staff and a highly skilled police officer. He was later to become overall head of West Yorkshire crime division.

Let me tell you that major crimes such as Mary's murder are never filed away undetected permanently. They are revisited from time to time and re-examined. Scientific technology is advancing all the time. In 1998 my friend and colleague Detective Inspector Chris Binns revisited this investigation. Chris is like a *Jack Russell terrier* with a bone – he never lets go. He utilised new sophisticated DNA technology to re-examine some of the original exhibits of this murder case and a DNA profile was successfully lifted from one of the crucial exhibits. The problem was there was no name to go with the profile. We had the killer's DNA profile, but did not know who he was. Brian hand-picked a small team of dedicated officers to form a new murder enquiry team to identify the killer. All the staff were of the highest calibre with good track records. He invited me to be a supervisor on the unit and I gladly agreed.

I moved to Shipley police station where our new incident room was to be located. Some people think murder enquiries are all about excitement and intrigue. The fact is, they can be dull and monotonous too. This was the case for the first month of this enquiry. We had to recreate the original incident room and rebuild it by hand.

The first investigation had taken place before the computerised HOLMES system had been brought into use and was comprised of a non-computerised manual system. Now we had to painstakingly examine thousands and thousands of documents and exhibits and educate ourselves on every tiny piece of evidence from the original case. The same too with all of the several thousand people who had been spoken to in the course of the original enquiry. We had to be familiar with their connection to the case. Our task was daunting, but we felt sure the killer would have been amongst the 9500 people interviewed at the time and we were prepared to go back and interview each of them again. The other problem was that more than 20 years had elapsed since the murder. It was going to be an enormous task to trace people who had been interviewed in 1977.

Brian had selected his team of seven – five detectives and two civilians – to perfection. Our main task was to obtain DNA samples from each of the original interviewees. The samples would be examined in the forensic laboratory, and would either eliminate them or identify one of them as the killer.

Many of the nominals had since died and others had moved around the country or emigrated. We had a system of dealing with all eventualities – those who were deceased, we were able to screen through samples from relatives. Overseas nominals were subject of a package dispatched through Interpol for completion by whatever countries police force they were now in. The vast majority of the nominals lived in the UK and they fell to me and my partner, Detective Nigel Spencer, to deal with. Nigel was a very astute Yorkshireman and a skilled detective. Not a lot got past Nigel.

We organised our time by doing local interviews intermingled by visits to regional areas in the UK. We were often away from home for weeks on end. We visited every police force area in the UK, clocking up more than 20,000 miles in the process. Some people knew they had nothing to fear and willingly gave us their DNA samples. We also came across some strange people who would not entertain us at all. Some would not talk to us or provide the sample, others would shake and sweat profusely. We always managed to get a sample from them either by sweet talking them or by threatening them with arrest. In fact, there was only one person we were not able to get a sample from, no matter how hard we tried. This man was convinced we were not on a murder enquiry at all, but wanted his DNA so that we could clone him. Why on earth we would want to clone him, I really don't know. One of his type was more than enough. We wasted a lot of time on him, but we managed to eliminate him in other ways.

After we had obtained the sample from these difficult individuals, Nigel and I would look at each other and have a little side bet on whether we had just spoken to the killer.

In April 2000 we received a notification from the forensic laboratory of a DNA hit. A local man, aged 24 years at the time of the murder and now, aged 47 years, was linked to the crime by DNA. He was actually still living close to the scene of the attack. At the time of the murder he had been working as a builder on a large project in Shipley, building a new Inland Revenue depot. He had been routinely interviewed along with 800 other workers from the building site. Now, a divorcee, the man had lived with his grisly secret for years. Perhaps he should have known the writing was on the wall and justice would eventually catch up with him.

Our investigation was very much high profile. He would have seen us record scenes for a crime reconstruction BBC television programme called Crimewatch close to where he lived. If he was expecting a knock on his door, he certainly didn't show it when I went to arrest him in the early morning. I knocked on his door awakening him from his sleep. I identified myself, showed him my warrant card and said – "It's about the murder of Mary". He went white, gulped and let out a loud fart… The long arm of the law had eventually caught up with him and he eventually admitted the crime.

During his questioning he said he had decided to go drinking that day and had met Mary on the canal towpath. She spurned his sexual advances and he had attacked her. He sexually assaulted her, strangled her, dragged her body to the river and threw her in. He was sentenced to life imprisonment. It was good to be able to bring some degree of closure and justice to the family of Mary and they really appreciated it. Her husband Bill sadly did not live to see it. In 1981 he had suddenly died from a heart attack at the same spot where his wife had been killed. He had never got over her murder.

CHAPTER 27

THE 'BRONX'

Having spent 18 months investigating the Shipley towpath murder I was now back at Eccleshill police station. The local authority owned housing estate of Thorpe Edge was blighted by the scourge of addiction to serious class A drugs such as heroin. Families were being poisoned by it. Strong addiction to the drug was ruining people's lives and causing an increase of other types of crime by people wanting cash to feed their habit. Drug dealers make a fortune for themselves by dealing in other people's misery. They are even prepared to supply free drugs for the short period it takes to get the user addicted.

I became aware of a block of flats in the middle of the estate where drugs were being sold as a large-scale business. It was in reality a heroin shop. Customers were queuing up at the door to buy their heroin wrap fixes. I raided the flat a few times on search warrants, but without any great success. The drug dealers just re-grouped and started dealing again. They were following a method of dealing that had been copied from the Bronx area of New York. The door and windows had been strengthened and fortified by steel plating. Builders blocks had been cemented by the door and steel girders placed as barriers across the door to prevent the police gaining entry.

Even on the warmest summer's day an open fire burnt in the living room. The purpose of the fire was twofold – the first to signal to customers that the shop was open for business by the smoke from the chimney and the second was to burn any drugs before the police could gain entry in the event of a raid. That is exactly what happened on the few occasions I led raids on the shop. The dealers thought they were beyond the reach of the law.

On one unsuccessful raid I took the opportunity to place covert type cameras inside and outside the flat before we withdrew. After placing the covert equipment I watched as the dealers took up residency again. Using the latest technology I was able to sit in my office and watch and listen to events taking place in the heroin shop. I heard one of the dealers say the flat could be bugged and he used a scanner device to search for electronic bugs. My heart was in my mouth – I thought I'm going to lose all this expensive equipment. Luckily, either the scanner or the person using it was totally inept and the covert equipment was not discovered.

Over a period of two weeks I watched everything that happened at the flat. There were two main dealers and they had a small number of trusted associates to help. One dealer opened the shop in the morning and stayed until late afternoon. Then the other dealer came on duty and kept the shop open until midnight. I could see them cutting up their heroin on the table and placing it into wraps, ready to be sold. A spy hole in the door allowed the dealers to vet punters who knocked, wanting to buy heroin. When the order was placed and accepted, the cash would be pushed through the letterbox and then the heroin passed out. From my camera outside the door I could see a steady stream of customers – sometimes even queuing – to make their purchases. Young men and women – some with children in their arms – feeding their dangerous habit. I was of course able to identify the dealers and their assistants as well.

I now had enough evidence to prosecute the dealers and close the shop down. I wanted to make the arrests while all the dealers were in the flat. I needed to make a rapid entry to arrest them and to seize the evidence such as drugs, cash and customer lists before it was burnt in the fire. That left me with the problem of getting through the fortified door fast. I got the idea of using a metal cutting chainsaw to cut a hole in the door. My team would quickly climb through the hole and arrest the gang.

On the day of the planned raid everything was in place, a convoy of police vehicles stood by, waiting for my order. A spotter officer watching the cameras told me all our suspects were now in the flat and I gave the order over the radio – "Go, go, go!", and the convoy set off. The officer with the metal cutting saw was in the back of the van with all the safety gear on. The plan was he would start the saw as soon as the convoy got close to the heroin shop, ready to open the door in seconds. Unfortunately, as he tried to start the saw it would not start. Try as he might, he could not get it going. I had to make a quick decision and shouted – "Abort, abort, abort!" over the radio and the convey deviated away from the flat and returned.

A telephone call later and a chainsaw engineer was being escorted by blue lights to our convoy. He got the chainsaw going again. I wasn't going to risk failure on the second occasion, so I told the officer to set off in the van with the chainsaw engine still running. The noise from the back of the van was something like from the 'Texas Chainsaw Massacre' movie. The plan worked perfectly, we managed to get into the flat in seconds, securing the arrests and seizing all of the evidence we needed.

The gang were perplexed when they saw the evidence we had and they were forced to plead guilty to hundreds of offences of drug dealing. They received a total of 23 years imprisonment. I got tremendous feedback from the residents of the estate for ridding them of the scourge of the heroin shop dealers who thought they were untouchable.

In January 2001, I moved to Bradford Central Police Station

at The Tyrls in the city centre where I took up the position of detective sergeant on the Bradford Area Drugs Unit. The smart suit, shirt and tie had to be put in the wardrobe and it was jeans and T-shirt for what was mainly covert type police work.

Drug dealers are very clever in covering their tracks and avoiding arrest and prosecution. It has to be a fast and aggressive way of policing to deal with them effectively. Give a drug dealer five seconds and they will dispose of the evidence and walk free. Our unit was effective in smashing the 'Dial a Dealer' drug dealers, so common in the Bradford area. They operate by giving their mobile phone number to drug addict customers. The drug user rings the number and in a secretive coded manner would order their requirements of heroin or cocaine. The dealer arrives in his car at an arranged location and the deal is completed in seconds through the car window. We were able to get the dealers numbers and break their secretive code of ordering.

We would pose as an addict and place an order for heroin or cocaine using slang words 'brown' or 'white'. One of our team, dressed down as a drug addict, would then wait at the arranged location for the drug dealer's car to arrive. The dealer would come to a halt by our addict and we then had seconds to act.

From my observation point, once I was satisfied it was the dealer, I would shout – "Strike, strike!" on my radio. One of our cars would then race in and block the front path of the dealer's car whilst another would block his rear, preventing him from driving away. In those split seconds the dealers would try to swallow the drugs to prevent us getting the evidence to charge them. We pre-empted this by attacking their car with our batons and smashing the windows. We then grabbed the driver or dealers in the car and arrested them. It was vital we managed to seize the drugs and their mobile telephones. It was a fast, exciting and dangerous way of busting the dealers. This effective method was used by us so often, it became like shelling peas and we dealt a serious blow to drug dealing in the area. We were sending dealer after dealer to prison and confiscating their assets of cash, cars and mobile phones thereby preventing them from easily returning to their wicked way of life.

Overall I don't think for one minute we – as a society and police force – are anywhere near to winning the war against drugs. We are just about keeping a cap on it. Some people call for drugs to be de-criminalised and they believe it will solve the problem. It won't, it will simply make it worse. It's akin to saying it is alright to go and break into peoples' homes because we cannot stop the burglars. By all means, we should treat addicts for their health problems, but drug dealers should be recognised as the killers they are and jailed for life.

CHAPTER 28

THE NEW DI

I had been a detective sergeant for 10 years, it was probably the most enjoyable period in my police service, but I wanted to better myself and get promoted. In and amongst dealing with murders and other serious crime, I had managed to pass the two exams required for promotion to the rank of Inspector. In August 2001, I sat a third and final interview before a board of senior officers. I successfully passed the board and in September of that year I was promoted to the rank of Inspector. I immediately applied for a further board to be a Detective Inspector and I was also successful in passing that test.

Another leaving party, another inscribed vase, and I felt sad to be leaving my DS role and the excellent team of detectives around me. As I had also passed a board to become a Detective Inspector, I was going to remain within the ranks of the CID, albeit at a different division. The police love to keep you moving, it's rare to get promoted and stay in the same division. It helps you from getting set in your ways and can prevent possible corruption by getting too familiar with people who would wish to corrupt you. I felt justifiably proud when I lined up in the Chief Constable's office and he shook my hand and said – "Congratulations, Detective Inspector, you are going to Keighley division". Having completed the obligatory newly promoted Detective Inspector course in October 2001, I was on the road again to a new division. Keighley division is located on the outer fringe of the force area on the border with Lancashire and North Yorkshire. It is a large Yorkshire town with some idyllic small towns and villages dotted around it. It also has a large rural aspect and its moors are popular with tourists and walkers.

At that time the police station was situated in the centre of the town. It was commonly regarded that Keighley division was the poor relation of all the divisions in the force. That was reflected in the state of the police station. Most of the other divisions had state of the art stations, whilst this was an old dilapidated building. The staff had made an effort to make my office presentable, but it was still a shit tip. The officers worked in bad conditions, but they were used to it. I was pleased to see my friend and colleague Nigel Spencer, who I had worked with on the Shipley canal murder, was one of my staff. It was always nice to see a friendly familiar face at a new division. They were all a happy bunch of people and they just got on with their jobs. Later, after I had moved on, a new police station was built in the town.

I was now a senior police officer and terms such as Sgt and first names to address me had gone. I was now a 'Sir'. In the CID, as staff got to know me, they would call me 'Boss' or 'Guv' when they saw I did not object. Previously I had been responsible for a small team of detectives, but now I had managerial responsibility for the whole CID department and other police plainclothes units in the division. I now carried the can for any increase in crime numbers and trends of any particular crimes. If a spate of robberies took place for instance, I would have to devise a response to deal with it.

The DI is more office bound. As a DS I was out there leading the team, but now I would only get out to supervise the most serious of incidents. I was checking files for evidence and making decisions whether to charge people or not. On the computer I was checking the crimes on officers' workloads and seeing if they were being properly dealt with. I was directing officers to gather evidence, show photographs, conduct identity parades, examine exhibits etc.

I was overseeing hundreds of crime investigations at any one time. As a manager, I now also had to attend a multitude of meetings – event planning, performance checking, tactical meetings – I was required at them all. A senior detective has to be available 24-hours a day. I was part of a small number of fellow DIs who worked on a 24-hour call-out rota to cover all of the Bradford divisions. This included every station in Bradford North, Bradford South and Keighley. On occasions we would also extend our cover to even include the Halifax area. Covering such a large, busy area meant it was inevitable that I would be the busiest man in the world. The system we used meant I was on call for a continuous seven-day period, day and night. This would come around every six weeks so in between it wasn't too bad. It was a demanding week when I was on call, no social life whatsoever. A continuous 168 hour week dealing with the most stressful crime situations that anyone could imagine. Not many other people would have to work such long hours.

I would have liked to have had more time to find my feet and settle in at Keighley, but I never got the chance. I thought I had come to a quiet Yorkshire town, but it was more like the Wild West. Two large gangs were feuding, they were basically fighting for criminal supremacy in the town. In particular, they each wanted to run the towns' lucrative drug trade. In a few months the gangs had been linked to 34 serious crimes such as shootings, woundings, assaults and kidnappings. Worse still, there had been three murders, one of them a 16 year boy who had been shot in the street in broad daylight. And these tit for tat killings and attacks were not about to stop just yet.

Soon after my arrival at Keighley I was on call. It was nearing midnight when I got the call that there had been another murder. This was my first murder to investigate as a senior officer. For the very first time I felt a little nervous and apprehensive as I made my way to the scene. The body of the victim was still in situ at the main roundabout into the town. To preserve the scene I had the whole road closed. It was to remain closed for the best part of 24-hours and it caused serious traffic congestion in the area.

A 24-year-old man had been playing football at the nearby sports centre. He left the centre in his car, not knowing that he was being observed by members of an opposing gang. Two cars followed him and as he reached the roundabout they rammed into his car, forcing him to stop. He managed to run away, but was chased by the others. He stumbled and they attacked him. He suffered 28 separate stab wounds and died from an axe wound to the head.

I spent the following eight months as the deputy senior investigating officer on this huge, complex and difficult murder enquiry. My senior officer was a detective superintendent called Phil. I had known Phil since we had been young detectives and I had and still have the highest regard for him. He was very calm and level-headed, and he was determined to sort the gangs out and bring the killers to justice.

Because it was gang warfare, we got no help from anyone in the gangs' immediate community. If we were going to get a result, we were going to have to achieve it the hard way on our own. We took over 800 statements and examined about 1200 exhibits. We traced 160 motor vehicles and seized a large number of them.

Eventually, after the most difficult murder investigation of my career, we managed to convict seven defendants in connection with the murder. They received a total of 69 years in prison.

In the aftermath of the trial the violence subsided and Keighley was a safer, better place to live. My baptism of fire at Keighley had boosted my reputation and made me a confident and well thought of senior detective. After one year at Keighley I got the opportunity to work at another Bradford division. For ease of travelling I jumped at the chance of moving closer to home.

CHAPTER 29

LAWCROFT HOUSE

In October 2002, I took up residency as the Detective Inspector at Lawcroft House police station at Bradford North. In contrast to Keighley, it was a modern state of the art police station. The facilities were great and we wanted for nothing. It is a fortress-style station built in the middle of the inner-city Manningham area. There was good reason that it should be fortress-like because the area had seen some of the worst civil rioting ever witnessed in the UK. In July 2001 racial tension between the city's Asian groups and the white population had been stoked up by extremists on both sides. The tension boiled over into large-scale rioting and many shops and other properties had been destroyed, 300 police officers had been injured and 297 persons had been arrested.

In the aftermath of the riot, jail sentences totalling 604 years had been given out. 64% of the residents local to Lawcroft House were of South Asian ethnicity. Policing at Bradford North in the wake of the riots was pretty much like walking on egg shells daily for fear of starting another large-scale disturbance. This sensitivity did not hold any pressure over me or how I went about my work.

I had never been unfair or biased against any group of people in my career – and how could I be, I was part of a minority group myself.

I already knew several of the staff at Lawcroft House and had worked with some of them previously. My fellow Detective Inspector was Shaun Berry who I knew very well. Shaun and I worked well together for a number of years. We both had an approachable style of management – we complimented each other and achieved great results. I think because it was such a difficult division to police, the staff in all the different departments came together as a cohesive unit and worked really well as a team. CID, plainclothes units, uniform patrol, traffic, PCSOs and civilian staff all came together. It was the best overall teamwork display I have seen in the police.

I had day-to-day management of detectives, proactive plainclothes units, specialist traffic officers and civilians. Jean Ginn and Sarah Joseph were both civilian Crime Clerical Officers who did a great job in keeping the division's complex crime administration system in excellent shape and made my life a lot easier. I also supervised the crime work of all the other officers in the division. I devised and implemented local training programs. I also devised new more efficient processes for how we dealt with the interviewing of suspects and how we achieved a good detection rate through scientific hit identifications by fingerprints and DNA.

I was destined to spend the next six years at Bradford North. In that time staff came and went – the majority of them were excellent; a few were not so good and I was glad to see the back of them. My bosses came and went as well. Again, some of them were great and a pleasure to work with. I had a policy of my very own throughout my career – learn from the good work of others and don't replicate the bad work of the useless ones.

In that period, I worked for a while for my first time under a female, newly promoted DCI called Ingrid. Some people thought she might struggle in the macho world of CID, but she was actually one of the best bosses I have worked for and she proved the doubters wrong. It seems a woman's cool head and ability to multi-task is a useful ability in the police service.

Whilst I was managing the crime workload of the whole division, I wasn't exactly achieving a hands-on approach very often. I was doing my rounds of daily planning, briefing and management meetings. Now it was only the most complex investigations that I was directly involved with.

Dealing with unexplained or suspicious deaths is a job for the Detective Inspector. There was scarcely a day in all my years as the DI that I did not find myself at the scene of some poor soul's demise. As you would expect, this type of incident can occur at any time of the day or night. Often I would just be watching a film on the TV or in bed asleep in the middle of the night when my mobile phone would ring and I would be told – "There is a body, boss". Again, often I would be able to resolve the matter in a few hours and decide it was not suspicious. Having climbed back into bed, only to be told by another control room operator – "There is a body, boss".

I have been highly trained in crime scene investigation and I have a vast experience of dealing with such incidents so I always felt confident as I made my way to the scene, that I would be able to deal with it and get to the bottom of what happened. When I was on call, I was always ready to go at a few minutes' notice. My clothes would be left out and I would have shaved before I went to bed, knowing I wouldn't have time if a call came through in the middle of the night. I had my all-weather box in my car holding weatherproof clothing, footwear, a torch and a forensic suit. One body scene could be in a living room and the next on a remote moor.

My first instruction would always be – "Protect and preserve the scene until I get there". No one would be allowed to enter that area unless I had authorised it, and then they would have to be suited and booted – in other words, wearing forensically safe clothing. Modern technology is so efficient and accurate that even one small stray hair carried into or out of a crime scene can be crucial.

The sixth sense warning that I had previously irregularly experienced, had now become a regular occurrence, often at the scene of a serious crime. The vast majority of deaths I attended transpired to be non-suspicious and from natural causes. You have to treat them all from the outset as a potential murder scene or else an investigation could be spoiled. If, for instance, a body had been found in a house, I would start my examination from well outside the scene. The garden would be checked for blood or discarded or hidden weapons. The doors and windows checked for evidence of a forced entry and the position of the locks noted. If the victim was known, I would have them researched and find out everything about them. I would have the address researched too and anything linked to the address such as a motor vehicle or other persons researched. The more knowledge you have the better informed you are to make a judgement.

If information came back that the victim had recently been the subject of threats, was involved in illegal drugs or had some other dubious history, then I would tread even more carefully. Dealing with deaths was part of my professional life and I would not be timid about it. I would physically handle and examine the body to search for injuries or cuts of any kind. Not nice, especially if the body had been there for a long period.

If I could not be sure that there had not been foul play, I would err on the side of caution, and I would call out the murder bandwagon – my detective superintendent, forensic experts, pathologist, scientist, search teams etc – and prepare for a long shift. It was not unknown to work a straight 24-hours, get six hours sleep and be back again in the incident room.

On occasions when I was of a mind to decide that death was straightforward, my sixth sense would click in and there was several times when I acted on my sixth sense and was proven to be correct. Of course, this feeling had no sensible reasoning of dependability about it. It was my private guide and I kept it to myself. Police officers deal on fact and evidence, not on feelings, and yet I found it a great help to me.

CHAPTER 30

UNDERCOVER

In my early days in the police I spent a lot of time working in plainclothes – often jeans and sweater – and I looked nothing like a police officer. My hair was quite long and I spoke with a distinctive Irish accent. There was more chance of me being mistaken for a gypsy than a police officer. In those days the method of using undercover cops was quite lax. Unlike today where specially trained officers are deployed and a colossal amount of regulations, guidelines and well-developed processes to manage them are in place in what is a highly dangerous area of policing. This really can be a case of 'sleeping with the dogs' and there is a big risk of getting bitten by the fleas.

Probably because of my appearance I was picked to do an undercover operation. A West Yorkshire criminal was suspected of committing a series of armed robberies on commercial premises. When he was making his getaway from the latest robbery in a stolen car, he injured a pedestrian who just happened to be in the wrong place at the wrong time. The enquiry team were trying to collect as much evidence as they could, but it was proving difficult. The suspect was now in custody at a police station in Manchester on a totally separate and unconnected charge. I was asked if I would pose as a prisoner and spend a night in the same cell as him. It was thought there might be a chance the suspect would talk about his escapades as some criminals tend to do to impress others. I agreed. Such a secretive deployment for obvious reasons would only be known to a senior officer. The officers on the ground had no idea that I was one of them. At the Manchester police station, they booked me in as a petty thief and they treated me like one. They put me in the cell, threw a dirty blanket at me and left me. As far as the staff at the Bridewell Police Station were concerned, I was to spend the night in the cell before going to court in the morning.

There was an open shared toilet in the cell. My fellow prisoner was not too pleased to see me as he had been disturbed on my arrival whilst doing his business on the toilet. I thought of asking for some air freshener, but this was definitely not the time for jokes. If he didn't like me as a fellow thief, what would he think of me if he knew who I really was. I tried to engage him in friendly conversation, but he didn't want to know. He just stared in a menacing and threatening manner at me. My sixth sense was calling out loud and clear – 'Don't turn your back on this guy'. And so I kept one eye open on him all night and I was one relieved and very tired officer the next morning when the jailer threw two slices of dry burnt toast and a cup of milky tea at me.

My other experiences of undercover policing were more successful. They came later when I had been promoted and I was concerned in the planning and management of the operations. Many of the undercover jobs concerned the supply of large amounts of drugs with values of hundreds of thousands of pounds. One slip in these operations, and the ruthless criminals would not hesitate to kill the undercover officer.

Some other undercover jobs were less dangerous and concerned ordinary members of the public who were going through a stressful or traumatic period in their lives and who hopelessly overreacted to it.

A young married couple living on the outskirts of the city seemed to have everything going for them. Both had good jobs, a nice home and nice cars each. They socialised with friends and all seemed to be well. The young lady started to act suspiciously by working late and going out with unknown friends. The husband became suspicious, kept a close eye on her and discovered she was having a secret affair with one of her work colleagues. This is where the usually decent, law-abiding young man deviated off the track of life and completely lost his way – he decided to have his wife killed. He hatched an elaborate plan to hire a hitman to kill her, while he had an alibi. When she was dead, her unfaithfulness would be dealt with and he would also inherit a large sum of money from the insurance payout.

Like all good detectives, I had my ears and eyes open through informants in the criminal underworld. I became aware of this plan and I managed it. It would be wrong of me to go into the intimate details of how I managed it here, it would serve no useful purpose, but could jeopardise future police operations. The operation ran for weeks and weeks. The husband was given every chance to withdraw from his quest to have his wife murdered, but he was adamant she should die.

The night of the planned murder came. He provided the hitman with a photo of his wife, told him where she would be at a precise time and even gave instructions on how she should die. He created an alibi for his own movements and then went home and watched television. He didn't know the 'hitman' was actually an undercover police officer and his conversations had been tape recorded. He waited at home for the police to call and break the news to him that his wife had been killed. The police did knock on his door, but, unfortunately for him, it was me. Instead of breaking the news he had expected I told him I was arresting him for soliciting to have his wife killed. The colour drained from his face and his whole world collapsed around him. He got a lengthy prison sentence and his marriage and good character lay in ruins.

A similar job I dealt with again arose from a common set of circumstances which was totally mishandled by the man involved. The man was a senior member of the medical profession. His marriage had broken down and his wife was going through the courts to reach a financial settlement with him. While he was happy to separate from his wife, he was not at all happy to have to part with some of his cash to her.

Any normal person would come to a resolution through solicitors or the courts, but once again this normally placid and intelligent man took the wrong road, he decided to have his wife attacked by hiring a hitman. Again, my sources warned me of the danger to the lady and I stepped in. For weeks and weeks and meeting after meeting with the ' hitman', the husband was adamant the woman should be seriously assaulted. Little did he know that the hired thug he was talking with was in fact an undercover police officer and his evil wishes were being recorded on audio tape. He told the undercover police office he wanted his wife to be seriously beaten. He wished for her legs to be broken and to sustain brain damage. He offered to pay £2000 for this 'work' to be done. On the day of the planned killing he waited for news of his wife's death. The 'hitman' called him and said the job was done. The husband answered – "Good".

When I arrived at his home and arrested him a few minutes later, I could almost visibly see the disappointment in his eyes. He was sentenced to 5 ½ years' imprisonment and his 30 year career as a health professional ended as he was struck off.

CHAPTER 31

ARSON AND DRUGS

The offence of arson is a difficult crime to investigate successfully because, by its very nature, some of the evidence is destroyed by fire. Depending on the gravity of the offence, I would always seek professional forensic assistance, which could include police specialist forensic officers, Home Office scientist and fire service experts. Damage to property is a serious enough criminal act, but when lives are lost, it is a terrible and most distressing crime.

I was awakened from my bed in the early hours of one morning to reports of a big fire in the city. A woman and her young son lost their lives in the blaze which had been started deliberately. They were trapped in the upstairs bedroom when the fire was started by someone using accelerants downstairs. A witness saw a youth running away followed by a loud explosion. I was at the scene very quickly. It was a most distressing thing for the emergency services to have to deal with, and also for the neighbours and friends of the victims who looked on helplessly. As a result of good scene management and investigation, the culprit was later identified and convicted.

Just prior to Christmas in 2004 I attended the scene of a serious fire in a small block of flats at Thorpe Edge. The sole occupant of the affected flat – a 43-year-old woman – died in the blaze. The fire had started inside the front door and the smell of turpentine was obvious. The murderer had used some plastic tape to cover the spy hole in the door so he could not be seen from inside. He had then poured the turpentine through the letterbox and set it on fire. The door was the only way of escape for the poor occupant so she sought refuge in a bedroom. The fire quickly spread, giving the unfortunate victim no chance of escape. She was trapped and died in the flat.

My initial enquiries revealed two men in a nearby flat had some type of grudge against the woman and I treated them as suspects from an early stage. Most fire engines are fitted with CCTV cameras and when I studied the recording of one of the fire engines in attendance at the fire, I could see the victim being carried from the flat by rescuers and being treated outside by paramedics. I could also see the two suspects standing outside, laughing and smirking and seeming to be getting some pleasure from events as they happened. A full murder investigation was launched and the two suspects were arrested. They were linked forensically to the fire and they then both admitted the offence. The two men aged 43 and 46 years were sentenced to life imprisonment.

Not all fire-related deaths are a criminal act. Some are accidental and some, tragically, caused intentionally by suicide. It can be difficult for a detective to work out which one it is.

In June 2005 on a quiet morning in Undercliffe, members of the public were confronted by a gruesome and frightening sight. A 22 year old woman engulfed in flames and described as a human fireball dashed from a house into the street screaming in pain. Some brave members of the public went to her aid and tried to help her. She suffered 80% burns and died in hospital several days later from her horrific injuries.

I got to the scene very quickly and saw her terrible burn injuries. I also got a strong smell of petrol. My enquiries revealed the victim was a native of Pakistan and was seeking asylum in the UK. She had a disturbing background that tended to make me look carefully at the circumstances of the incident. She had encountered terrible discrimination in her home country because she had converted to Christianity and had embarked on a relationship with a man who was not acceptable to her family. She had been threatened and abused and was very frightened. She fled to the UK to seek safety and a peaceful life as she wanted to live it. Just prior to the fire she had received a letter from the Home Office inviting her for an interview. She wrongly assumed she would be sent back to Pakistan and she panicked. She poured petrol over herself and using a lighter, set herself on fire. Before she died of her injuries she actually recounted this to the police and nursing staff. It really was an awful tragedy and a terrible way to die.

The vast majority of fatal incidents I attended were not caused by any third party. Each of them still demanded a good initial investigation, to be certain that I had arrived at the correct conclusion. Some were more difficult than others.

On a cold February afternoon I had to go to Chellow Dene Reservoir where the body of a 57-year-old man was recovered from the water. I quickly ascertained he was a psychiatric patient from a nearby hospital. He had run away from his escorts and waded into the deep water of his own accord and drowned.

It's surprising how many people die from falling down stairs. As an investigator it is hard to know if the person fell, or tripped, or was pushed. It's made even more difficult when there is a background history of violence, drugs or alcohol abuse in the home. I have attended at several such deaths and resolved them all successfully.

One in particular caused me a great deal of suspicion. A middle-aged woman had died after falling down the stairs at her home. She and her partner had been drinking alcohol most of the day and they were known to argue. Despite this suspicious background, I did not receive any type of my sixth sense vibes to warn me that anything untoward had taken place. I was satisfied then, when I found a young boy in the home, who had been present and was able to corroborate the account that she had fallen by accident.

Deaths from unlawful drug overdoses are commonplace. Sadly, the majority of them are young people because in the main it is young people who are addicted to drug abuse. I have never come across any of these victims having been forced to take the drugs. They have taken them of their own free will. However, the person who supplied the drugs or who facilitated their use by the victim is criminally responsible. The untimely deaths of these young people leave their families and friends devastated. Many families are expecting that knock on the door from the police at any time because of the chaotic lifestyle of their son or daughter. Other families are completely taken by surprise as they never suspected their offspring to be using illegal drugs.

In a 7 day period in 2007 I investigated seven such drug deaths and consequently attended at each of their post-mortem examinations. All the deaths were caused by illegal drug usage – a bad batch of heroin was doing the rounds in the Bradford area and it was simply poisoning the users to death. I was attending so many scenes and at the mortuary so often I didn't know if I was coming or going. I gave warnings through press interviews to the TV and newspapers pleading on drug addicts to take special care. Some people thought I was being a bit naïve making an appeal to drug addicts, but I had to do my best and I hope the warnings didn't entirely fall on deaf ears.

In January 2003 I had some respite from attending crime scenes when I was temporarily promoted to the rank of Detective Chief Inspector. The crime manager was on long-term sick leave and

I was selected to take his place. For the following nine months, whilst I performed the role, I was somewhat frustratingly confined to my office. Any downtime between meetings was spent number crunching – trying to find ways of increasing the detection rates, reducing the crime numbers and at the same time reducing spending on staff and investigations.

I was subjected to grillings from the force command team who seemed so besotted with statistics that the human impact of our work seemed to be totally overlooked. The senior officer who conducted the divisional reviews was an ignorant pig, full of his own self-importance. He was quick to criticise everything being done in the division, but never had the expertise or capability to offer any positive advice or direction. He was only concerned about his own year-end productivity bonus payment. As one can imagine, I was only too happy to return to my DI role in October and back to dealing first hand with serious crime.

The majority of crime is committed by someone related to the victim or close to them in some other way, such as a friend or neighbour, for example. I would always start to investigate a crime from the centre, starting with the husband, wife, family member, and extending right out until I was satisfied they were all in the clear.

In June 2004, I was called out late one night to the Queensbury area. A 21 year old man was deceased in the living room of a house with apparent head and facial injuries. I pieced together his movements from prior to his death and discovered he had been drinking and taking drugs. His brother had been with him at some points of the day and he had also used drugs. I tracked the brother down to another address in the village and spoke with him. I wasn't happy with his account and he was arrested. He later admitted to killing his brother in an alcohol and drug fuelled attack.

In May 2006, I was again roused from my bed to a stabbing at Keighley. A man and woman had had a domestic argument. The man had got a kitchen knife and stabbed the woman a number of times. He then turned the knife on himself and stabbed himself once in the abdomen. When I arrived, the woman was in a comfortable condition in hospital and the husband was stable in another ward. There was not much for me to do, everything had been done properly, so I left it in the hands of the night uniform staff and made my way back home to bed. I hadn't been asleep very long when I got another call to tell me it was now a fatal incident. The husband had encountered unexpected complications with his injury and had died. Back out of my bed, and off to Keighley again for another long shift.

In June 2006 I received a call of a serious stabbing in the Holmewood area. A 14 year old girl had received a horrendous injury when a large knife had been plunged into her stomach. She was extremely lucky to survive the incident and later went on to make a full recovery. I spoke to the girl's mother and a young boy who had witnessed the attack. The person responsible was the girl's step-father, who had attacked her for no apparent reason. He had run away from the scene and we followed the direction he had gone. He had disappeared into a wooded area, but with the help of X-ray 99 – the police helicopter – we located him hiding in a field and arrested him.

CHAPTER 32

FATAL TRAGEDIES

At 12 noon on one Saturday in June 2007 I was getting ready to go see Bradford City's football match at Valley Parade; it was reasonably quiet at work and I planned to take the afternoon off. However, my plans had to be cancelled when a call came in of a stabbing in the White Abbey area of the city. Neighbours reported hearing a disturbance coming from a house. The woman of the house had then run into the street chased by her partner, who was armed with a large knife. They watched in disbelief as he plunged the knife into the woman killing her instantly.

When I arrived, we traced the assailant to a relative's house where he gave himself up to arrest without any resistance. I was then busy dealing with the murder investigation all day. I finally got home for a few hours' sleep at 2am the following day. I never even had the chance to look up Bradford City's result. I should have known better than to make plans when I was on call.

In October 2007 I went to the Canterbury area where the body of a 40 year old man lay on the street. I quickly established the 16 year old son of the victim was responsible for stabbing his father to death. I made contact with him by telephone and encouraged him to give himself up immediately.

One can only imagine the utter devastation and grief that engulfs a family when one of their number suffers a violent and unexpected death. This sense of grief and shock is doubled when it transpires that another family member is responsible. Family loyalties are tested to the limit and some families never fully recover. From a police perspective, violent crimes – where the offender has no connection whatsoever to the victim – is much harder to deal with and to resolve successfully. Sometimes it is simply a matter of the unfortunate victim being in the wrong place at the wrong time. We call it a stranger crime.

One dark October evening in 2003, a 31 year old man left home to walk to his local club for a social night out. By all accounts he was one of the nicest, gentlest persons you would wish to meet. On the way he stopped at an automatic cash machine and withdrew some cash. As he got close to his social club at Undercliffe he was unfortunate enough to meet two young men who were intent on violence. They were in fact two violent drug addicted thieves who were intent on robbing someone to get cash for the next drugs fix. They violently attacked him, punching and kicking him and hitting him with some wood. They stole his cash and mobile phone before running away, leaving the unfortunate man to die.

Because it was a stranger attack, we had no idea who was responsible and a large-scale murder enquiry was commenced. I again teamed up with Detective Superintendent Phil from the Keighley murders investigation. It was a long and difficult task, but we managed to identify two suspects within a few weeks. The stolen mobile phone proved to be the key element in leading us to the killers and they were arrested. The whole murder team worked their socks off to detect this horrible murder, but none more so than my competent workaholic Detective Sergeant John (Mugsy) Maguire. Not only did he get murder confessions from the defendants, but he also detected dozens of other crimes they had committed.

The pair admitted the killing, saying they had set out that night to rob the first person they met to get money for drugs. That first person could have been anyone. Two vicious killers were deservedly taken off the streets for a very long time.

An 87 year old man was crossing the street one busy lunchtime in Idle village when he was hit by a car. The car failed to stop leaving the old man dying in the road. With no witnesses able to give details of the car, it could have proved impossible to trace. Amongst the debris at the scene, I found a small piece of glass from the headlamp of the car. We painstakingly researched the piece of glass until we identified the make and model of the offending car. I used the media to appeal for information about anyone who had a similar car that might be damaged. The appeal paid off and we received a tipoff about a similar car in the area with damage consistent with being involved in the fatal incident. I traced it and arrested and charged a 30 year old man.

At 11pm one night in May 2006 I received a call regarding the violent death of a 37 year old disabled man who had been driving his car in the Manningham area of Bradford. He was turning his car when two passing men got into an argument with him. As he got out of his car they grabbed his walking stick from him and used it to assault him. The driver died at the scene. I spoke with several witnesses at the scene and, as a result of their information, the two men were traced, arrested and charged.

The aftermath scene of a fatal road traffic incident is always an upsetting and distressing event. It is not a pleasant sight even for the most hardened police investigator. With CCTV cameras now covering most of our everyday movements in public the facility is often available to examine the CCTV tapes and watch the incident take place.

On a dark evening in March 2007 I was called to Manchester Road where a 17 year old pedestrian had been struck by a car and died. It was evident from the carnage at the scene that the car must have been speeding. I examined the city's CCTV system and discovered the incident had been caught on camera. I could see the young man crossing the dual carriageway road carefully. Two cars could be seen travelling down the road at great speed and obviously racing each other. The victim had no chance because of the speed of the car that hit him and it was terrible to watch it happen. The driver failed to stop and tried to cover his tracks, but we arrested him later that night and charged him.

At 5am one morning in December 2008, I was called from my bed to attend a horrendous fatal car crash in Killinghall Road. Four young men aged 15, 16, 17 and 21 years had tragically died at the scene. The car they were in was a high-performance car that had been stolen earlier. A police patrol car fitted with an on-board CCTV recording camera had spotted the stolen car just before the crash. By checking the CCTV recording I could see the crash as it happened. The car was travelling at an alarming speed. The driver lost control on a slight bend and the car crashed into a commercial premises and exploded into a fireball.

The police officers did their best, but they were unable to save the young men, such was the ferocity of the blaze. Their families were devastated when they heard the news. It also had a bad effect on the police officers who were involved with the incident. We may get hardened to dealing with such tragedies, but we always feel the associated grief as well.

CHAPTER 33

SEXUAL OFFENCES

Sexual offences were a common part of my work. I was hardened to most crimes because I was dealing with them so often, but still some were so terribly sickening that I would never forget them.

On a beautiful sunny day in July 2004, an 85-year-old woman was out walking in the suburbs of Bradford. Because of her age and poor health she became lost and disorientated. She approached two builders working in the area and asked for help. One of them, being a good Samaritan set off in his car to visit local elderly residential homes to see if she belonged in any of them.

The second builder turned out to be a convicted rapist. He enticed the elderly woman into his van on the pretext of taking her home. He then took her to an isolated lane where he violently raped her. The victim was later reunited with her family and then reported the incident to the police. I attended the scene with a team of detectives. It was hugely difficult to get a coherent account from the victim because of her age and condition, but an experienced female detective conducted the most sensitive interview with her and managed to get a full account of the incident.

I traced the offender and he was charged. He denied the offence, but he was linked to the crime through his DNA and he was found guilty at the Crown Court. I made a media statement suggesting that he should not be released until he no longer posed a threat to the public. The trial judge condemned his violent crime and sentenced him to prison for the whole of his natural life. I kept in touch with the old lady's family for some time and I know that she never fully recovered from her ordeal.

In October 2008, I dealt with a case of sexual grooming of a child over the internet. A 36 year old man had befriended a 14 year old girl on the internet. He arranged to meet her and sexually assaulted her a number of times. He was sentenced to 6 years imprisonment.

I have dealt with dozens and dozens of rape offences each of them varying in circumstances and gravity. Regretfully though, I have to say I have dealt with a high proportion of allegations that were investigated fully and proven to be false allegations. There are many reasons why a person would want to make such a serious false complaint. Often it was just spite or revenge. Sometimes it was to cover up to a boyfriend or husband for a now regretted consensual sexual encounter. Other false complaints emanated from people with serious psychological defects which are often difficult, if not impossible, to spot.

Some sexual allegations never had any hint of truth in them whatsoever. A 12 year old girl complained of being abducted by three men in a car and taken to an area where she was sexually assaulted. You can imagine how seriously we treated such an allegation. After three days of full-scale investigation by a team of detectives, the victim's account was crumbling. She was interviewed again by specially trained detectives and she admitted she had made the whole story up for no good reason. She was cautioned for wasting police time.

Sexual allegations can be easy to make and difficult to disprove. That is why it is necessary to investigate them fully and professionally so as to be fair to everyone concerned. The people who make such false complaints do no good whatsoever and serve only to undermine the genuine complainants of such a serious crime. A wrong accusation can destroy the lives of innocent people. The recent high profile cases of the Coronation Street actors Michael Le Vell (Kevin Webster) and Bill Roache (Ken Barlow), where they were found not guilty of several serious sexual offence charges, highlighted this to the watching nation. Many people were of the opinion they should never have been charged in the first place.

As a senior police officer, I had to make similar decisions as to whether an accused person should be charged or not. I was well aware of the standard of evidence that was required to justify taking a case to court and I ensured the case was fully investigated from every angle before I decided on the outcome. This meant looking closely at the complainant's account and seeking corroboration from other sources such as witnesses and forensics.

Although this procedure has served us well in the past, recent events are imposing changes in the system and, in my opinion, may be influencing the decisions to charge and prosecute some of the current high profile celebrity cases. The Jimmy Saville episode, where he allegedly sexually assaulted many people over several years without prosecution, raised questions about how such cases were treated. Many people felt the victim was ignored whilst the high profile suspect could get away with it. In the face of such public criticism the police and CPS appear to have altered their evidential charging standards and got their knickers in a right old twist. They must realise they will never be able to please everyone – especially the media. They must investigate each case to the highest professional standard and then be guided by the evidence, and not by the individuals involved.

Personally, I am all in favour of letting our tried and trusted judicial system, in the form of a judge and jury, examine the evidence in detail and rule on a 'guilty' or 'not guilty' decision. The police and CPS should gather and evaluate all the evidence, but, in the end, if the complainant stands by their account, they should have their day in court. It is totally wrong though that the potentially false victim is able to remain anonymous whilst the accused person is hung out to dry for all to see and in the process possibly destroying their lives.

The system of trawling for further victims of the accused person by identifying them through the media is also fraught with danger. In effectively advertising for victims, the door is opened for even more miscarriages of justice.

The high profile cases currently in the spotlight have highlighted problematic areas in dealing with sexual offences and hopefully this will lead to a thorough review of the system that will be fair and beneficial to all of the community.

CHAPTER 34

TRAFALGAR HOUSE

In March 2008 the Bradford police divisions were restructured and boundaries moved to fit with electoral wards. I was transferred to the CID department at Bradford South. I was based at the new Trafalgar House police station at Nelson Street near the city centre.

Again, new bosses, new colleagues and new CID staff to work with. Although it's fair to say I did know most of them and had worked with some of them previously, I felt lucky because for the most part I had inherited a strong, enthusiastic and hardworking unit. The younger detectives were particularly keen and enthusiastic and were led by equally professional sergeants. I practically had to order Sgt Jagsy and his epitome young detective partner Sean to go home sometimes – they were so keen to get to the bottom of serious crime and bring the offenders to justice.

The police organisation is no different to similar large units in other walks of life. The vast majority of staff are dedicated, hardworking and efficient, but there is always one or two who are shirkers, lazy and good at hiding behind other workers. In every unit I worked in I kept on top of their performance measuring data and let it be known to them that they would shape up or ship out and I encouraged a few to move on elsewhere.

I was always able to get the best out of my staff, not by using the big stick, but by encouragement, training and appreciating their efforts.

Lazy or incompetent police officers may be few and far between, but they can be a real problem to resolve successfully. Left untouched they can destroy a team and be a source of frustration to their hardworking colleagues who have to cover for them. There is a process in place to deal with such officers, but it is largely ineffective. The process to deal with unsatisfactory officers is cumbersome and complex. It relies on management staff to understand the process and having the courage to implement it.

The civilian personnel officer and the business manager has a big part to play in this, but, quite frankly, I often found them sadly lacking in resolve and expertise. The officer who is performing at an unsatisfactory level will always win out against such ineffective opposition. I have seen such officers take up to 6 months paid sick leave for some highly suspicious medically indeterminate reason such as a bad back or stress – effectively, withdrawing their labour or going on strike, when their performance has been questioned by a line manager. It is almost unheard of that such workshy officers would ever get dismissed. Instead, the best a manager could hope for is to move them along to be someone else's problem.

A low performing police officer is one thing, but a senior officer who is not up the high standard required for the job is a much more serious affair, and I came across several of them in my time. They are in a position of power and can have a negative influence on a lot of staff and on how a department or division is run. Some are amateur psychologists who read a deep library book overnight and then think they know all the answers. They talk about 'blue sky thinking'. They want to eliminate crime by painting the walls blue and making people eat less chips and burgers. Sadly this thinking does fool some people and some officers gain promotion on the back of it.

The pace of the job did not slow down in my new role at Trafalgar House. The crime kept coming in thick and fast. Some people think there are hundreds of police officers on duty at any one time, waiting in the police station to turn out at the drop of a hat. They would be surprised and perhaps would not sleep too easily in their beds if they knew the actual reality of police numbers. There is simply rarely enough officers on duty to cope with the demand at any one time. People often have an unrealistic expectation of ringing the police and seeing them arrive in a few minutes. It cannot happen because there is often no one to respond to the call. The situation is steadily getting worse as more cuts are made to police resources. Calls are graded to allow for a more rapid response for the most serious of incidents. Dialling 999 to report the loss of your car's tax disc will not result in a police car with blue lights flashing outside your door in two minutes. In fact such a call does not merit a police visit at all.

In the future I can foresee the public's perception of the police response will have to be re-educated and changed. With heavy demands on the service and fewer resources, more and more people will have to report minor crime and anti-social behaviour either online or by going to the local station and joining the queue at reception.

On an average morning at Trafalgar House, I would come on duty at 8am and study the overnight incidents. At 9am I would brief the staff and allocate work for investigation. More often than not, there would be more incidents to be dealt with than available officers and I would have to allocate several incidents to each officer. It was of great concern to me that I might be overloading them to the point that they would be unable to give their best attention to each job or put too much pressure on them, but what else could I do.

One morning's fairly typical example list of incidents to be allocated for enquiry and managed to a high level was:

2 x males in custody for serious assault

1 x male in custody for an offence of rape

4 x men in custody found driving a high-powered car stolen in a burglary

1 x attempt murder by discharging a shotgun at a man

1 x indecent assault on a girl

4 x cars stolen overnight

8 x offences of house burglary

This workload had to be managed against the Police and Criminal Evidence Act (PACE) clock, which dictates timescales for prisoners in custody. Everyone was fully employed and it would be a long day. Bad news though for any member of the public who might have been expecting a routine call that day, it would have to be cancelled.

The season of goodwill doesn't exist in the world of many of our customers. A Christmas murder or two could almost be guaranteed. One Christmas morning I came on duty hoping to be able to get home for my Christmas dinner at lunchtime – no chance of that. An unexplained death of a 20 year old man report waited for me. There was a shooting where the windows of a house had been blasted with a shotgun. There was an arson report, several burglaries and car related crime, and a sexual assault on a six-year-old girl to deal with. There was something even more tragic about the murders I attended at Christmas. At a time when most people were happy and celebrating it was heart-breaking to see the pain and anguish that some unfortunate families had to deal with. What would my neighbour Mikey Boran back in Ireland make of all this. What a different lifestyle to his quiet, peaceful life on the farm. Sometimes I couldn't help but think that maybe I should have stayed there too…

Irrespective of how busy I was, there were some calls, which simply could not wait. I had to drop everything and go. A dog walker had found a body lying on an icy footpath in the Toller Lane area. I took Sgt Jagsy and Sean from their already busy schedule with me to investigate the circumstances of the death. It took most of the day to resolve and it transpired to be a natural death. Standing in the cold the only thanks we got was to be pelted with stones by the local youths. Later that night I found myself at the scene of a fatal stabbing of a young man in a normally quiet rural village near the Yorkshire Moors. A young man of excellent character and from a loving family had intervened to bring peace to a pub disturbance and was fatally stabbed. The killer was arrested and sentenced to life imprisonment. I was at the scene all night, but the locals kept me fed and warm with an endless supply of hot coffee and cakes. Typical of police work – no two days are the same.

The media play a hugely important role in detecting crime. It's true to say it can also fuel the fear of crime through reporting and sometimes sensationalising it. As a senior police officer I received an excellent level of training in media matters. I worked on courses with journalists and broadcasters. I practised camera techniques, earpieces and studio situations. A 30 second slot on a TV news channel could resolve an investigation that would otherwise drag on for months – such is the power of the media. I often appeared on local TV news programmes, giving details of some serious crime and asking for information or sometimes giving my reaction to an important court sentence for a job that I had dealt with.

I would be contacted every day by reporters looking for exclusives or even fillers – short crime items – to fill their pages. My name and face was plastered over the local papers on such a regular basis that I became somewhat of a local celebrity. From my early days of being an anonymous police officer I was now recognised everywhere I went. The chief crime reporter for the local daily newspaper was a man called Steve Wright. As we were basically both in the crime business, we knew each other well. Steve could be a right pain in the ass – always probing, looking for that exclusive angle. Having said that, he helped me tremendously by giving me publicity and he probably solved more crime than the average detective.

An elderly woman had been attacked in her home in the Eccleshill area. The intruder had assaulted her and then used her dressing gown belt to tie her up. It was a shocking crime and I wanted to do all I could to arrest the man responsible. I arranged to do a TV press conference from outside the scene of the attack. For best effect it is good to have something to catch the TV viewers' attention and we decided I would hold the dressing gown belt so that viewers could see it. At the last moment I realised I could not use the belt as it had to be preserved for forensic examination. On my way to the interview I stopped off at my house (my wife had a similar dressing-gown) and I borrowed the belt for the TV cameras. Close to a million viewers saw my wife's nightwear on the news that evening – sometimes you just have to improvise.

The media are very good and will work with you and support you to get the best results. Of course they get free print or a page filler, but the value to an investigation cannot be understated. You do need to be extra careful in everything you do or say or you could end up looking foolish. The media like to use exciting and catching sound bites and statements to jazz things up. They would simply love you to look at the camera, scowl and say to the suspect – "I will track you down". Not a good idea – for one, it is making it personal and, secondly, if you don't track him down, you've got egg on your face.

A young man contacted the local newspaper to complain of police harassment by my officers. He said he was being stopped regularly and the police were treating it as one big joke. They had even taken to writing 'HA' on the bottom of each search record, and he felt they were laughing at him. I went to see him to try and resolve his complaint. I pointed out he was a prolific and active criminal. He was breaking into cars and houses on a regular basis. I told him he was high on our priority list to stop offending. We would disrupt his criminal activities as much as we could, and that meant stopping and checking him on a regular basis. He agreed with me that some action was indeed justified, but he said – "There's no need to rub it in by writing HA on my forms". Smiling, I had to point out to him that 'HA' was actually an abbreviation for 'Hotel Alpha', the name of our division, and it appeared on every form.

CHAPTER 35

OUT OF LOVE

On a Monday night in May 2008 I started my first of seven consecutive days on 24 hour call, I was hoping for a quiet week, but I didn't really believe it would be quiet. I was right. At 1:20am I was awoken by my first call of the week. It was a call that brought me to a crime scene from hell. A gang-related murder had taken place in the Manningham area. One man was dead at the scene, another was badly injured. The offenders were believed to be still in the area and a large crowd was gathering. In addition to the murder there was a serious risk of public disorder.

It was important to protect the scene for forensic examination, so my first instructions were – "Secure and preserve the scene and I will be in attendance very soon". I was on the road in my car within minutes. Every few minutes my mobile was ringing from one senior officer or another asking me to expedite. I knew it was a delicate and complex incident from the outset and I knew the purpose of the calls was to place the monkey firmly on my shoulders. Once the others had passed the book to me, it became my responsibility and they could take a step back and breathe a sigh of relief.

The situation that met me at the station was chaotic. I then went to the scene and took charge. It took some time to establish what had happened, the specific details were sketchy at that stage, but I was able to determine that two opposing groups of men were involved. There had been an earlier altercation during the evening when one of their cars had its windows broken. They arranged to meet each other in the early hours of the morning to talk. The meeting erupted into violence with the two occupants of one car being attacked by six or seven men. Two of them were armed with guns and the others had bats and sticks. Both men were assaulted and stabbed. One of them died at the scene.

Six persons were identified as possible suspects and I had their houses visited by armed officers immediately and they were arrested. Each of these houses had to be preserved and searched as crime scenes. In addition to this I had about 10 of the casualties' families brought to the police station to be interviewed. Understandably, they were all upset and agitated and difficult to manage. From an initial scene of utter chaos I was now beginning to gain control and bring some semblance of order to it. Although I'd had very little sleep, I was not tired. In these circumstances, the adrenaline kicks in and helps keep you going. I got my first quiet moment at about 5am that morning and I reflected on what I had done and on my ongoing priorities.

In that moment I realised I was falling out of love with this working lifestyle. Like the vast majority of other senior police officers, I should be at home tucked up in my bed and not trying to manage this stressful and demanding situation. After 29 years in the job I realised I was getting burnt out and maybe it was time to leave it to someone younger. The job was also taking its toll on my health, I had been diagnosed as a diabetic about 20 years earlier and I was on insulin injections several times a day. That was difficult to manage when I was virtually working night and day. My radio crackled with yet another problem to resolve, so I put my own welfare thoughts to the back of my mind and carried on.

At that time a dedicated homicide team had been created in the force. The system was that they would move in later that morning and take the murder enquiry from me. It was a professional unit with some great detectives attached to it. If I'm totally honest, I have to say, I was not impressed with some of the senior investigating officers on the unit. They were not career detectives like me, they were butterflies moving from one department to another simply to build a wider portfolio for their CVs. They lacked experience and directed investigations by going through an A to Z checklist of things to consider in a major enquiry. As I handed this murder investigation over later that morning, I realised that not only was I getting tired, but I was getting frustrated at what I saw as a lack of expertise of others. It was definitely time to look for another career path. My problem was there was not a lot of opportunities open to me that I would be interested in. Then I spotted an advertisement for a vacancy for a Detective Inspector in the North East Counter Terrorism Unit.

CHAPTER 36

INTERNATIONAL TERRORISM

The North East Counter Terrorism Unit (NE-CTU) was set up in 2007, one of five counter terrorist units in the country; it was born from the Special Branch (SB). Its purpose was to strengthen the response to the threat of international terrorism.

The world was witnessing a surge in brutal terrorist attacks – mainly from the Al Qaeda extremist organisation. Although atrocities were taking place all over the world, it was known the United States and the United Kingdom were the main terrorist targets. The 9/11 attacks in New York in 2001 had seen almost 3000 people murdered. Closer to home, the London bombings in July 2005 had seen 52 people lose their lives. Other attacks had taken place over the world and many others had been foiled by the police and other security agencies.

The Special Branch had been in existence at the time of these atrocities. Their work was shrouded in secrecy and many people just did not know what they did. Special Branch was reorganised in 2007 and called the Counter Terrorism Unit to make the public more aware of the terrorist threat and to provide a point of contact for all terrorism-related issues.

I had very little experience of the Special Branch or of anti-terrorism work, but I decided to apply for the advertised post. I completed the long winded and detailed application pack and waited. I knew there was interest from several other officers who had also applied. I was given a date for my formal interview and I researched everything I could find about terrorism, its origins and causes. I looked at the main players, organisations, and the multitude of government initiatives and programs to deal with it. Even with all my police experience I had to work very hard. At the back of my mind was the constant effort to achieve success and be the best. I was interviewed by the head of the unit and one of its most senior officers.

I was somewhat surprised when I was instructed to bring photo identification, such as my passport and proof of my address along to the interview. I'd been working for the force for 29 years – were they still unsure of who I was? The panel were great and put me at ease before launching into the interview. I came out of the interview quite relieved that it was all over and feeling quietly confident. I got a notification a few days later that I had been successful; in fact, the unit commander told me that it was one of the best interviews he had ever conducted.

I gave my notice in at Bradford South, although I knew it would be some time before I actually made the move. The vetting process for getting into the CTU is one of the most stringent and testing procedures in existence for any job. You have to be squeaky clean and of the highest integrity because of the delicate and sensitive nature of the work. My whole family and circle of friends were examined. My bank accounts were examined in detail. I was asked if I gambled or drank alcohol, what newspapers I read and what I looked at on the Internet. I had nothing to hide and I was confident I would pass the vetting procedure.

Then one day out of the blue I had a telephone call from the CTU personnel officer. She told me they were unable to appoint me. I couldn't think what the problem could be so I asked. I was dumbfounded when she said – "It's because you are Irish and have an Irish passport". I was so shocked, I could hardly speak. I said – "How can you discriminate against me because of my nationality!" It was then it struck her also the enormity of what she had said. She became flustered and stammered – "Those are the rules". To be fair to the personnel officer, it wasn't her decision. While the other senior CTU officers kept their heads down and left it to her, she had been naive enough to be the one to give me the message.

Obviously, I kicked up a mammoth fuss. The force was bending over backwards to show what champions of diversity they were and here they were caught with their pants down, blatantly refusing me a position on the sole reason that I was an Irish citizen and not a British subject. If they had done this to an Asian officer for example, they would have risked a riot.

Several letters were exchanged with senior police officers over the next few weeks. They were embarrassed by the problem and I could tell they wished it would go away. They didn't want their highflying careers to be tarnished with that unsavoury word – discrimination. I had enough experience to know that, when you challenge a rule within the Home Office or the police organisations, you come up against faceless bureaucrats and it is very difficult to beat them. In the end I was offered the opportunity of becoming a British subject at their expense, and then taking up the post. My Irish culture is important to me and I would not relinquish my Irish citizenship for anything. We came to a compromise where I became a dual citizen. I am now an Irish and a UK citizen and I can use either passport.

And so, eventually, on 1 January 2009 I was on the road again to a new place of work with a whole new set of colleagues and staff. For security reasons I cannot say where I was working, it was not in a police station, but in a commercial environment. I had a large team of CTU officers under my command and we had special responsibility for the safety of the aviation industry. We were entrusted in keeping the travelling public who fly all over the world on business and leisure safe from terrorist attacks.

Dealing in national security, my work was of the highest secrecy, I learned a whole new secret language because CTU officers speak in code. If you could listen in to a conversation, you would still not know what it was about. I was in daily contact with colleagues all over the world. My patch was now considerably bigger than Bradford or indeed, West Yorkshire. I had regular contact with colleagues in various other national and international intelligence agencies. My role required me to travel a lot. I was also a regular visitor to New Scotland Yard. The sense of history in that building is almost tangible – at times I half expected to meet that great fictional detective Sherlock Holmes walking down the corridor. I couldn't help thinking I had travelled a long road from my Irish farmyard to Scotland Yard.

One of my biggest difficulties in ensuring the safety of the flying public was in my dealings with airport operators and airline operators. The aviation industry is a cut-throat business and their primary concern is to make money. Keeping the public safe costs time and money, something the operators begrudgingly do because legislation forces them to do so. All I can say is thank goodness that safety legislation exists and it is enforced rigidly upon them.

Again, for security reasons I cannot go into detail of the work I was involved with. The threat level to the aviation industry is currently rated as substantial. The work of the CTU is highly instrumental in keeping the public safe from terrorist atrocities, and we were highly successful in doing so. We cannot ever publish our successes, except those disclosed in high interest court cases. Rest assured, there is a team of highly skilled and motivated people working away in the background to keep you and your family safe from the threat of international terrorism.

The threat from international terrorism has not gone away and we will have to live with it for many years to come. We have officers from the CTU and intelligence services all over the world to thank for suppressing the extremists who would destroy us all, if they got their way. I fear in the future the terrorists may turn their attentions to softer targets – countries such as Ireland. Every country needs to be alert to the threat. History has shown that peace can be achieved, but that will require dialogue and political good-will from leaders of the future.

Extremism is the curse of the modern world and extremists lie behind most of the problems we encounter daily. If you are extreme in any way or another, it will cause problems for you or for someone else. Water is good for you, but if you are extreme in its use, it will harm you. Eating a MacDonald's meal is pleasant, but if you are extreme and eat them for every meal, they will eventually kill you. It's the same with religion, for many people it's a way of life and provides hope and support to them. However, if it is pushed to extremes, then it can have a detrimental effect.

The obvious answer, in my humble opinion, is to make your way through this world by doing everything in moderation. Maybe we should send everyone to jail who is an extremist in anything whatsoever – but hang on – now I'm being extreme!

The CTU was a whole new way of working for me and I enjoyed it immensely. I wish I had made the move earlier in my career. It had its problems though and wasn't the integrated smooth running hub it should be. Departments were over-secretive to each other with many of its staff on self-motivated ego trips. Others known to me as OC, WT, GG and LW were selfless in their devotion to keeping the public safe and highly professional.

In May 2012, after more than 32 years in the police service, I decided I had done enough and I retired. One big final leaving party, another engraved piece of cut-glass, and I was down the road.

Eccleshill Police Station

Lawcroft House Police Station

The Square, Castlecomer

Trafalgar House Police Station

Epilogue

Over the years I have maintained my strong connections to Ireland. I have spent a fortune travelling back and forth. I'm not quite sure why, because the country never did anything for me and I resent the fact that its sons and daughters are still its biggest export. I also worked wonders for the Irish economy by telling my friends about the beautiful country and encouraging them to go visit. Bord Failte, the Irish Tourist Board, should make me an honorary member for my contributions to Irish tourism.

The Ireland of today is not the country I left in 1973. The boom years of the Celtic Tiger have been and gone. We are now in a deep recession and emigration is once again a huge issue. My town of Castlecomer has lost its main employers in Comer Yarns, The Products, The Brick factory and the Caravan factory. No major employers have replaced them. Maybe it's a measurement of the recession to see that its 10 public houses are now reduced to only 4. It is still a beautiful place to live and visit. The local Discovery Park provides an educational insight into the history of coal mining in the town along with beautiful walks through its demesne.

The roads infrastructure throughout Ireland has improved greatly through the use of EU cash. Immigrants from other countries, particularly Eastern Europe, are replacing our own youth who are emigrating around the world. I would not dissuade anyone from emigrating, if it is necessary to do so. Wider opportunities are available in other countries – go get them.

For me the most striking difference is the increase in violent crime. For a small country violence is rife and murder is now commonplace – human life is getting cheaper. The ranks of the Garda Síochána are being reduced because of financial restraints at a time when they should be increased to deal with violent crime and to protect its citizens.

Of course the big positive factor is the peace process in Northern Ireland. Who would have thought it could ever be achieved. The peace process shows what can be achieved against all the odds and is a lesson to other troubled areas in the world.

My parents and my disabled brother and sister have passed away now. When I lost my parents, my connection to Ireland seemed to be lost forever, but I got over it and my wife and I are now more frequent visitors than ever. In fact, we now split our time 50/50 between Ireland and the UK. I have four of the best sons anyone could ever ask for. They are split between Ireland and the UK, so I have family wherever I go.

I now look back fondly on my long career in the police. I wouldn't change any of it and I have no regrets. I am proud of my achievements for myself and for my Irish background. My quiet rural upbringing was not a drawback to me, my sound childhood and family grounding kept me on the straight and narrow. Some of the things I have seen and witnessed were so upsetting and traumatic, they would knock any weak willed individual off-track.

After such a long and interesting career it was inevitable I would miss the job after I retired. My body clock still woke me very early, I still put my mobile phone beside my bed, but now it is quiet throughout the night – thank goodness! Most of all I miss the camaraderie of the good people I worked with. But, like everything else, I have adapted to my new quiet way of life and I am perfectly happy now doing very little and enjoying life to the full.

While I enjoyed my police career immensely, I'm not sure I would actually advise anyone to join the police force now. My time was easily the best era to be in the police. I saw it expand and develop to a high-tech organisation and my pay and conditions were reasonable. The current coalition government is wrecking the service with draconian recessional cuts. Pay and allowances are being cut, pensions are being reduced and officers will have to work much longer – perhaps to 65 years – to qualify for a pension. Policing is a young man's job, not for someone in their sixties.

The deadly dangers associated with the job and the high qualities of integrity and dedication makes the police service a special case. Who do you call when the brown stuff hits the fan – you call the police to pick up the pieces that no one else in society will pick up. Of course, not all is nice and rosy in the world of the Criminal Justice System and I feel reasonably qualified to give my opinion on its shortcomings. The cuts enforced by the recession will affect the efficiency of the police. Senior officers are doing their best to maintain the best uniform initial response, but this is at the cost of reduced crucial background staff such as detectives and forensic officers. A police service that only provides crime numbers for insurance purposes is not much of a police force.

Chief Constables, Divisional Officers and the local Police Commissioner should be more vocal and instrumental in opposing these cuts to the politicians and should be honest with the public about their negative effects. The reality is many of them are little more than political 'yes-men' who look after their own careers. There would be little chance of a knighthood or a post in the HMIC (Her Majesties Inspectorate of Constabulary) office, if that boat was rocked.

Still too much of a police officer's time is spent dealing with bureaucracy and pointless form filling. For example, every time you stop someone to speak with them you have to complete a form. The only reason I can think of is to satisfy the civil liberties brigade. Officers will spend hours and hours each day just waiting for a prisoner's rights to be exercised. Solicitors, social workers, appropriate adults and interpreters all have to be assembled before the suspect can be asked any questions.

Some police forces even take their officers off the streets to teach them how to speak a number of foreign languages, so the non-nationals they might interact with do not feel alienated. What's wrong with the immigrant learning English? I learnt very early on that integration is the key to a settled and happy community.

The Crown Prosecution Service (CPS) hold responsibility for who will be charged with serious crimes in the UK. They assess the strength of the evidence. If there is a realistic chance of a conviction and if it is in the public interest to charge, then they should allow the police to charge the suspect. Straightforward enough it may seem, but not always so in my experience. The CPS is influenced by factors which have a negative effect on its ability to be completely fit for purpose. They are not resourced sufficiently to be able to cope with their heavy workload. This results in poor court preparation and long delays in the prosecution process. Being oversensitive to government performance targets, they are reluctant to take on prosecutions that are contested or not 'nailed on' evidentially. This leads to criminals not facing prosecution and many of them that are charged are able to negotiate a lesser charge through plea-bargaining and still walk free. Where in this crazy world of targets and performance data is the victim's feelings taken into account?

You may have noticed I have not referred to the sentences given to many of the miscreants I write about. That is because I don't know what happened to them. I learned a long time ago that, when I arrested someone and charged them, then my job was done. No one tells you what happened to them unless you make an effort to find out or you read it in the newspapers. The justice system is so limp that in the end I would become frustrated when I had put a lot of hard work into a case to see the defendant get a smack on the wrist. No, whatever happened in court was not my responsibility and I left them to get on with it. That's not to say I don't have strong views about sentencing, because I do.

As a member of the public you are quite entitled to go down to your local Magistrates or Crown Court and watch proceedings. I'll be surprised if you come out not having reached the conclusion that the system is designed to be heavily in favour of the defendant with very little, if indeed any, reference to the victim. The defence solicitors run out their daily well used list of excuses – my client has had a hard life, he was drunk, he was on drugs, he had no money, he was provoked, he has the promise of a job…

The magistrate or judge will then follow Home Office guidance before handing down the sentence. That guidance will include the fact that at present the prisons are almost full, so try something else. Often they practically apologise to the convicted person and fine them a paltry sum of money to be paid at one pound a week. Some people need to be in prison for the safety of the public and for their own best welfare. They will not commit crime in prison, it gives them the opportunity of getting their lives back on track, away from the influences of drugs, alcohol and bad companions. Prison is the only punishment feared by even the most hardened criminal. They do not like it and they will do everything in their power to avoid it. But, importantly, the fear of prison will also make them think twice about committing the crime again. Anything less than prison is regarded as a let-off by the criminal.

The criminal justice system is not a good place for any decent law abiding citizen to be, whether as a victim or as a witness. The system is not sympathetic to their needs, it looks after the criminals. It's high time that the pendulum should strike the other way. All this may sound a bit depressing, but the actual fact remains that the police service and the criminal justice system is in a far, far better place than when I joined up in 1979. I'm going to do my bit to make it appear even more efficient and dynamic as my next project is to write a fictional novel based on my experiences and the people I worked with. I will ensure the baddies are put in their place by the system. Should be easy enough to do in a world of fiction! I'm off to Bollards Pub in Castlecomer now to contemplate this over a long pint of Guinness.

Mind how you go now.